# Practical Guide for Digital Marketing

Seven steps to engage your customers, get new ones, increase your sales, and build a winning digital marketing strategy

## Cláudio Torres

### Digital Enablers Books

www.thedigitalenablers.com

Copyright © 2018 Cláudio Torres

All rights reserved.

No part of this publication may be reproduced, copied or distributed in any form or by any means, or stored in a database or retrieval system or website, without the prior written permission of the author.

Digital Enablers Books

For my wife Eulalia, and kids David and Carina.

# CONTENTS

*Digital marketing is for everyone* ................................................. *1*

*STEP 1 - Talk* ................................................................ *25*

*STEP 2 - Interact* ........................................................... *41*

*STEP 3 - Tell* ................................................................ *53*

*STEP 4 - Push* .............................................................. *63*

*STEP 5 - Spread* ........................................................... *77*

*STEP 6 - Search* ........................................................... *87*

*STEP 7 - Track* ............................................................. *97*

*An Extra Step* .............................................................. *105*

*A practical plan* ........................................................... *127*

*Where next?* ............................................................... *139*

*Additional Material* ....................................................... *145*

*About the author* ......................................................... *147*

# INTRODUCTION

# DIGITAL MARKETING IS FOR EVERYONE

The Internet is no longer a new thing. We all use email, look at websites and buy on online shops, and most of us use social networks like Facebook or Twitter. However, it has become incorporated so quickly into our everyday lives that it is easy to forget an important fact: Our clients and customers also use the Internet. Maybe more than us.

Apart from using the Internet, you need to understand that consumers have taken it over. Social media, blogs, social networks, collaborative websites, and games, have changed forever the way customers relate to companies, brands, and products.

In the past, customers were focused on conventional media. They received information about companies and products via leaflets, newspapers or advertising. In all cases, the company had some control over their messages, either through public relations or paid advertising. Likewise, retail businesses used their physical point of sale as a powerful weapon to attract new customers.

But this has all changed quickly. Consumers now have mobile devices and powerful search tools, which can find products, services, or show them where the nearest shops are. Blogs, podcasts, and YouTube videos have become the primary source of information for many people, especially those who like to talk about brands and products and comment on their experiences. Social networks have become a constant channel of communication between customers who mention details about what they buy, how they use it and what they thought of it.

Also, it has never been easier to create an online shop. E-commerce has become so popular because any newly created company can compete on product and services sales against large commercial brands that have invested in well-located stores.

This can be a scary scenario for anyone who runs a business, and if you are struggling with the effects of the digital revolution on your market, be aware of using it to your advantage. If you had not yet come to this point, wake up before it's too late.

You need to make the most of the opportunities, created by the Internet and digital technologies. You need to be online to acquire new customers and grow your business. And meanwhile, you must work to avoid losing your current customers to new online competitors. For all these, I will show you a set of steps to fight back and put you in a winning position at the digital revolution.

To leverage the Internet for your business without wasting money or resources, and to establish a more permanent competitive advantage, you need steps that lead you to a coherent, efficient, and effective strategy for making the Internet your primary business ally - today, tomorrow and forever. This is the point of this book.

I use the term Digital Marketing in this book to highlight the fact that this is not about using sales and marketing concepts on the Internet or using one particular web site or another. What I am talking about is a new working model for setting your business up on the Internet. This is what we mean by Digital Marketing.

Digital Marketing is the combination of commercial, marketing, and promotional strategies, applied to the Internet and to the online consumer behavior. It is not about one particular activity or another, but a coherent and efficient combination of steps that build a permanent contact between your company and your clients. Digital Marketing helps your customers get to know your business, trust it and make the decision to buy from you.

## UNDERSTANDING THE ONLINE CUSTOMER

Digital Marketing is becoming increasingly important for businesses and companies, not due to technology but because of a change in consumer behavior. Consumers are using the Internet as a means of communicating, gathering information, maintaining their friendships and entertainment.

This is no temporary trend or something just for youngsters. Researches into the Internet shows that it represents a permanent change in behavior, a pattern that spans all ages and income bands and that equally affects all businesses.

Consumers look for information about products and services, not just to buy them, but also to find out what other consumers think about.

Recall your recent purchases. How many times have you used Google to find an article that compares products, analyzes or reviews different brands? The vast majority of consumers use the Internet as an information source to help them make their opinion about products and services before making their buying decision.

These days, information on the Internet comes from blogs, discussion forums, video sites like YouTube and Vimeo, collaborative sites like Wikipedia and social media. The content in most of these sites is provided by the consumers themselves, which generate updated information on just about any economic activity, product or service on the planet.

As people use the Internet increasingly for building relationships and communicating with friends, they are constantly exchanging ideas through social networks. These networks such as Facebook, Twitter and LinkedIn aren't just about exchanging information between friends, they reflect people's consumer experiences.

Social networks have a significant impact because they spread this information through multiple relationship networks. When a user writes something, that information can be transmitted virally through all the different groups of people who are linked with him. In social networks, a consumer is never isolated. A complaint or a compliment not only affects him and his friends but also all the friends of their friends, greatly enhancing the power of the message.

Of course, advertising is still a useful Internet tool. When customers are looking for information on Google, Bing or Yahoo, they are influenced by the ads they come across on the sponsored links. And when they use social media, they are affected by the banners and promotional videos they come across on the blogs, forums, YouTube and social networks.

However, it is important to note that only a small proportion of consumers respond to online advertising. Google figures estimate that less than 10% of people using their search facility click on sponsored link ads.

Email and other types of electronic message are yet another way of attracting customers, although thanks to spammers, scammers, and viruses, people are increasingly more selective about reading their emails. As a result, it is getting harder and more complicated to achieve good results from email marketing.

Finally, many methods and activities can be used to attract customers via the Internet, and it is necessary to use your research and planning to choose which to apply and to avoid throwing money away on ventures that do not get results. To make this easier I have developed a seven-step practical guide, which will help make your Internet activities efficient and allow you to analyze the returns on your investment.

## WHY NEED A PRACTICAL GUIDE?

In a speech from September 2008, Rudy Giuliani, the then Mayor of New York, said a phrase that became famous: "Because change is not a destination, just as hope is not a strategy." This had its intentions and political interpretations, but I use it because it exemplifies well what we are going to discuss.

A practical guide, made out of straightforward steps, as we present in this book, is a way to build and define a marketing strategy. And a strategy is not a document, not a plan, but a way to reach a goal, a destination. You can achieve a goal without any planning and yet have a strategy for it. Planning only organizes the approach and makes its execution easier.

So, a strategy is only useful if we have a clear destination. A strategy without a clear goal is like following any path without a destination. Or as Lewis Carroll, the author of "Alice in Wonderland," said: "If you do not know where you're going, any road will take you there."

And that's what many companies and brands do in marketing. They initiate digital marketing actions without having a clear goal in the hope that this will somehow contribute to their business. But as we mentioned in the beginning, hope is not a strategy.

So when I talk about a practical guide for digital marketing, I mean a way to achieve your business or sales goals through a robust digital marketing strategy.

Likewise, without a guide and a set of steps to implement a strategy, you are betting on the hope that something will work for your business. You can hire countless digital marketers to craft your website, an app, campaign on Facebook or Google. But without setting a strategy before and having a clear set of goals, all this is called hope. Your hope that by investing in a website, an app or in online campaigns you are reaching your connected consumer and attracting new customers.

What I mean is that all digital marketing techniques, widely advertised in many books, such as SEO, SEM, Inbound marketing, Mobile marketing, Facebook ads, Google ads, etc., are important and valid, but these are only actions. They are just tracks in your way, and if you do not know where you are going, any road will take you there.

So a digital marketing guide is your strategy that must precede actions and should be guided by the business and marketing goals of your business. Or to summarize simply: Define first where you want to get to (the goal), then how you will get there (the guide), to finally start walking (the actions).

## HOPE IS NOT A STRATEGY

With the digital revolution, it is no longer possible to think about detached actions on the Internet or on social networks. Whatever your business, surely a significant portion of your consumers are represented by connected users who access the web more than any other media. So, including digital marketing as part of your business planning, creating integrated actions that make better use of available resources, is critical.

The digital ecosystem has become an environment that affects your business in a variety of ways and will continue to change even if you do not invest anything in digital marketing. Unlike traditional marketing, where control is of the business and corporate media, in the digital ecosystem, the power is of the consumer. So even if you do not participate and are not connected, your consumers will be there, talking about your products and services, comparing your company with those of competitors, and finally looking for ways to relate to your brand.

If you do not invest in digital marketing, you will not only be giving up talking about your company to your consumers, but you will be opening the door for everyone to talk about your business without you being aware of or participating in the process. So, make no mistake: unlike other media, the Internet affects your business regardless of your will.

Investing in digital marketing does not mean creating a website, a blog or advertising with banners. A marketing manager at a mid-sized company with a well-built website told me that he once received a visit from a digital agency that wanted to sell him a Web 2.0 site, as if there were versions of websites, the Internet, or consumers and as if a new website puts your company on a new level of digital marketing. Nothing is further from reality, but it is common for companies to use new terms to push digital products to their customers. Of course, she did not sign a contract with the company.

The digital ecosystem is so vast and dispersed that separate and uncoordinated investments invariably mean wasted resources. You have first to understand the whole context of digital marketing and then plan coordinated and practical actions that are linked to one another, that is to say, one activity contributes so that the other one grows and get momentum.

If you read the digital marketing texts that circulate on the Internet, where each expert talks about what he understands, you will get the impression that digital marketing is advertising on Google and Facebook, or perhaps you think it's about creating a blog and a YouTube channel. Maybe they will tell you about SEO (Search Engine Optimization) or SEM (Search Engine Marketing). For sure, a company that works with mailing will say that the important thing is to invest in email marketing. Finally, some bloggers or influencers may mean that you should be constant in the media and social networks.

Although all of these actions are within the so-called digital marketing, you should consider the case matter to be much broader, and there is a need for a more systemic look at the question before investing your first dime on the Internet. It's like walking through the amusement park before picking out the toys.

So the keyword is planning. Without planning, you will spend a lot of resources, including money, before you understand what really works. The worst is that you will pay the most precious resource of all, time.

However, to plan, you need to understand what you are expecting, and what strategies you should consider in your planning. But when we talk about planning and strategy, people usually think about documents, meetings, and consultants. In fact, in most of the cases, a plan looks more like a guide that drives you through the necessary steps, and that is what we will work on in this book, planning as a set of steps to push you into the right digital marketing strategy.

## THE BEHAVIOURAL VISION

The first thing to understand is that we are still talking about marketing and consumers. When we talk about digital marketing, we are talking about people, their stories and their desires. We are talking about relationships and what needs are to be met.

It is common for businesses to think that because we are talking about the Internet, there is something new about human behavior. It is more common for some people to spread these ideas as if the question were the technology and resources to be used.

The consumer is the same, and his online behavior reflects the desires and values he brings from his experience in society. The changes come from the evolution of society, as in the case of consumer protection laws, which gave new impetus to people's desire for more respect and protection in the consumption relationship. When the consumer feels more protected, he exploits commerce much better on the Internet.

The significant difference is that some behaviors and desires were asleep or restrained due to the restrictions of mass communication and the pressure of modern society on the individual. What digital technology, in fact, did was to reopen the doors to individuality and to the collective, without the mediation of any interest group. People are themselves and meet according to their desires. They can find their peers in the crowd and create spontaneous and creative networks.

As mentioned before, when we talk about digital marketing we are talking about people, their stories and their desires. We are talking about relationships and needs to be met. Thus, the vision that most closely approximates reality is based on consumer behavior and considers that the online consumer is the same consumer, the same human being, who also watches television, reads newspapers or magazines, listens to the radio, works, walks and lives as an ordinary citizen. It's as they say: the Internet is made up of people. A behavioral view considers that the consumer is the center of the Internet and that their behavior, intent, desire, and needs are to be taken into account. A view based on consumer behavior considers that people are present on the Internet to interact in four primary activities:

- Relationship
- Information
- Communication
- Entertainment

This simple model shows the four behaviors of the online consumer and allows us to analyze in more depth and clarity each of the activities carried out on the Internet, as well as to understand the motivations in the use of each of the existing technologies. Using this model allows you to know that the consumer uses Google primarily to get information and not to find websites so it will pay more attention to content than advertising. There comes the need to create a content-based marketing strategy.

The behavior-based view also allows us to understand that the consumer is embedded in a social network to establish relationships and therefore is less susceptible to advertising than when faced with television. Hence the need for a relationship-based marketing strategy.

Thus, the view based on consumer behavior allows us to analyze and define marketing strategies much more appropriate to each of the environments and to each of the situations present on the Internet. This vision naturally leads us to the digital marketing model that will be presented here, a flexible and versatile model that adapts to the movements of the digital technologies and its innovations because it is not centered in the current technology or the possible activities in the web, but in the consumer who uses it.

## YOUR PATH FOR DIGITAL MARKETING

Constant innovation makes it hard to define models, and there are those who preach that the ideal is to have no model, ensuring that you are always adapting to reality and change. In practice, however, to allow the organization of effective marketing actions, you have to work with a model. Without it, strategic, tactical, and operational planning and activities become unfeasible.

However, a model may be flexible enough to survive changes and innovations and still fulfill its function. Everything depends on the center adopted for the model, that is, on the values on which it is based. In the book The 7 Habits of Highly Effective People, Stephen R. Covey talks about the need to establish a center for what he calls the Circle of Influence, in which we deal with our visions and values, and from which we adjust the lenses we used to observe the world.

According to Covey, the center is the source of our security, guidance, wisdom, and power, and the various centers that people adopt define their behavioral patterns and worldview. Finally, the author proposes that the most effective way to act is to place our center on our principles so we can adjust our lens for a more proactive and compelling vision.

Likewise, when we adopt a vision based on consumer behavior we are choosing the consumer as the center, we are placing it at the center of our principles. Business, marketing, communication, and advertising must be consumer-focused, as that is the only source that enables the company to survive, grow, and make lasting profits. Nothing is more effective than adopting a digital marketing strategy by having the consumer as the center of our circle of influence and looking at that lens, setting its behavior as the basis of our approach.

Thus, the digital marketing model focused on the consumer, and their behavior will be at the same time practical and flexible, mainly because it is based on correct principles and what really matters to the business and marketing: the consumer. This model shows that while the strategic, tactical and operational actions of a digital marketing campaign can be different depending on the company and each scenario, the marketing techniques that are based on consumer behavior are equally applicable to digital marketing, from which applied correctly to each of the environments and activities present at that time on the Internet.

However, with the digital revolution and the expansion of the digital ecosystem, it becomes difficult to use traditional terminologies, such as content marketing or email marketing. After all, are e-mail marketing actions, which follow the ideas of direct marketing, only applicable to emails?

And what happens with the millennium and Z generations, where email falls into disuse and comes down to the identifier of an account, or to formal communications? And would not it be the notifications (push notifications) of the apps, a new form of direct marketing?

But rather than strategies, the names traditionally associated with digital marketing today reflect specific actions within a more complete model. This model is part of consumer behavior and expands to activities derived from this behavior.

So we can summarize our consumer-centric digital marketing guide as a set of verbs and actions that reflect what a company or brand has to do: Talk, Interact, Tell, Push, Spread, Search and Track.

Let's briefly review each of these steps and their meaning: Talk means acquiring protagonism and saying something to one or more people, be prepared to hear questions and formulate answers eventually; Interact means connecting and interacting with others by sharing protagonism, talking, exchanging ideas and establishing a relationship; Tell means exposing an idea or story to a group of people; Push means to promote and increase knowledge of your products and services; Spread means to distribute actively and passively your message encouraging others to help and do the same; Search means look for information and data relevant to the brand; Track means getting and analyzing data to understand what is happening.

This approach leads us to our guide for digital marketing, with six steps focusing on consumer behavior, allowing us to define the activities to be carried out (tactical) and the technologies to be used in the implementation of the action (operational), creating an effective, comprehensive and comprehensive digital marketing strategy. The seventh step is related to monitoring and the need to keep up with constant evolution, while allowing for a robust and evolving model, accompanying changes in the digital ecosystem.

Thus, our complete model consists of seven steps:

- Talk: Actions related to the production and dissemination of content aimed at attracting the consumer.

- Interact: Actions linked to social networks to build a relationship with the consumer.

- Tell: Actions related to direct communication with the target audience.

- Push: Actions related to online advertising campaigns to raise awareness about our products and services.

- Spread: Actions related to brand message dissemination virally to expand brand reach.

- Search: Actions related to online surveys to know our market, our consumers and our competitors.

- Track: Actions to monitor the results of the steps and their constant updating.

To finalize our model to use digital marketing, we have to consider that, unlike conventional marketing, consumers are always inserted in various environments and contexts, in an interconnected and dynamic way. This means that each strategic action alone can and will interfere with the others, and in many cases, it is difficult to separate one action from another.

You should not think of the seven steps as stand-alone strategies or activities. Do not think about them as closed boxes. To understand the interdependence between them, you must think of each as the thread of a web netted by a spider. Although they seem more suitable for accommodating ideas and objects, the boxes are rigid and only provide what adapts to its format. On the other hand, the smart spiders have created, with their webs, a much more dynamic, flexible and at the same time resistant method to accommodate what interests them.

Although there are seven steps, each will produce various tactical and operational actions. Each action should be seen as a thread of the web being formed. Strategic steps guide the direction of the yarn, but it is the web assembly and the number of woven yarns that generate the consistency of the result.

Even though a spider web is made up of the main wires, which go from the center to the outside, it is only supported by the lines that run around the mesh, interconnecting and giving structure to the main wires. This also happens in digital marketing. It is the interaction between the various tactical and operational actions that produce synergy and generates effectiveness and consistency in the results obtained.

The spider web image illustrates well the concept of digital marketing, with its six strategic dimensions, with the monitoring to the center guaranteeing the monitoring and control of the results. This is also how the spider knows everything that goes on in the web because any movement in a wire produces a vibration in the center that informs the spider that it is time to act.

The web also illustrates another fundamental concept of digital marketing: the need for coordination and interaction between strategic actions. Thinking about a separate action is as fragile as the web of a spider when it is only with a few strands.

A newsletter works best if it conveys information related to the content generated by the brand, and social media helps spread the content and enhance its viral effect. And only with the monitoring of the newsletter, website, and social networks is it possible to understand the motivations of the consumer and the result of the newsletter sent.

All this interdependence between the actions of digital marketing allows us to affirm that the best way to plan your activities is to work with each of the seven steps in a coordinated approach, increasing the amplitude of each one and allowing one action to help to potentiate the other.

Thus, the construction of digital marketing should follow the example of the spider when it builds its web. It stretches a few main threads and then weaves from the center outwards in a spiral-like movement that at the same time increases the reach and strength of your web.

To summarize: To guide your digital marketing, you should think about a set of seven steps, each one creating actions, in a coordinated and interdependent manner, generating synergy and results.

# THE CUSTOMER CONTACT CYCLE

The seven steps cover the entire contact opportunity cycle that your business needs to have with its customers. To help you consolidate your vision of how these seven steps can help your business on the Internet, let's picture the complete cycle of exposure and communication your company has with your customers.

In a typical cycle, you talk about your products, producing content that captures your customers' attention when they are using search tools and looking for information to support their purchasing decisions.

To get the most out of this content, you Interact at social media and social networks, providing relevant information to others, thereby creating and maintaining a good relationship with people who have an interest in your business.

To leverage these networks you virally spread your message, magnifying your exposure well beyond your group of customers who have a direct relationship with you.

For more engaged customers you tell about your company news, effectively for feeding information via electronic mail.

Using online advertising, paid or free, you push the process of exposure, having a positive impact on new customers who are most receptive to it.

Throughout this steps, you also search about what customers want and need including those with whom your company doesn't have a direct relationship.

Finally, you track all your actions and results, which will provide you with information about the effectiveness of your digital marketing efforts.

The seven steps of digital marketing deal with this entire cycle: Talking, Interacting, Telling, Pushing, Spreading, Searching and Tracking.

By implementing these steps in an integrated way, your business will achieve a substantial presence on the Internet and will be able to secure a competitive advantage in this new era of the digital revolution.

## ABOUT THE E-COMMERCE

You may notice that I did not include e-commerce as one of the digital marketing steps. This could seem strange, especially if your business is involved in retail, tourism, entertainment, or any of the other sectors that have been affected by new online e-commerce businesses.

So, to conclude this chapter I will address e-commerce and explain why I do not consider it to be one of the digital marketing steps.

The idea of buying over the Internet is not new. Improvements in Internet security and the positive experiences of the many customers who have benefitted first hand from online shopping have driven the growth of the e-commerce market so that it now enjoys a considerable market share in many sectors.

Yes, customers are buying more and more online. But it would be wrong to assume that you will do big business by merely establishing an online shop on your website.

First, you should think of e-commerce as an additional point of sale for your business. A cheaper, more efficient point of sale, which reduces your space and stock requirements. Many online sales websites began as an additional sales channel for a company with a physical presence, like a shop.

If you have a retail business, e-commerce must be used as a channel to increase sales and help your customers to access your products.

But like any sales channel, you first need to analyze its viability and the impact it will have on your business. If you have a company that manufactures a product that is already sold in third-party stores or e-commerce partners can actually jeopardize your relationship with the market and undermine your pricing policy.

Second, it is essential to understand that the fundamental key to e-commerce is not marketing but logistics.

An online store does not sell by its own. You need digital marketing to help attract visitors and buyers to your online store in the same way it can bring them to your physical store.

But when buying online consumers expect to be served quickly and securely and to receive the product either online or delivered to their home. Getting this logistics right can be extremely complex, depending on the nature of your business.

Creating an online store without carefully first examining your sale, payment, delivery, and return logistics can expose your business and make e-commerce your enemy instead of your ally.

Think of a ceramic tile supplier. Ceramic tiles are bulky, complicated to transport and challenging for the customer to visualize online. That is why you don't see too many ceramic tile online stores.

For e-commerce to be feasible, the first step is to create a logistics model that enables the delivery of small quantities of the product to a broad geographical area at a viable cost. Also, you need to calculate the return policy and costs, in case your customer decides to send the whole order back because he thinks the real product color does not match what he saws online.

So, before hiring a company to build your e-commerce, it is imperative that you analyze in detail the full logistical process, including product presentation, choices, sale, payment, delivery, and return policy. Once you find a viable and profitable solution to each of these questions, you will be ready to build your online store.

And finally, before you start, be sure to analyze what sales channels already exist on the Internet. Often, partner with an existing online shop is the best option for many businesses.

Companies such as Amazon, Booking, eBay, Etsy, and Apple have great channels and partnership programs for businesses to sell online. Depending on your product or service, and the region you can supply, these large e-commerce solutions can provide valuable and highly effective solutions for selling your products on the Internet.

Furthermore, these large online stores can feed into your digital marketing strategy as they already invest heavily in attracting new customers.

Before any business makes its decision on e-commerce, it is essential to weigh up the investment and the risks of establishing an independent virtual store against the benefits of using an established online outlet partner.

# STEP 1 - TALK

## USING YOUR CONTENT

The first step you need to take is to talk about your business, about your brand, about your products and services, and even about the knowledge that you and your company have that is interest to your consumer.

A restaurant, for example, should talk not only about its activities, menu, and facilities but also about the gastronomy and culture it represents, including even some recipes or gastronomic tips.

But talk at the digital world means to first produce content, in the format of texts, images, podcasts, and videos, and then publish them in social media, and make them accessible to searches. Thus, this first step has three elements complement each other in the action of talking to the consumer: Content, Social Media and Search tools.

By social media, we mean all digital resources that to allow the collaborative creation of content and its sharing of information in various formats. These categories include blogs, collaborative content websites like Instagram, Pinterest, YouTube and various other sites that allow the individual or collective authoring, and the sharing of multimedia content.

Blogs are social media in which one or more people publish their content, and several others read and comment. There are millions of blogs around the world, and some blog websites like Blogger and WordPress. Another feature of social media is collaboration, in the sense of the collective creation and consumption of content. In this area, the most famous website is Wikipedia, a collaborative encyclopedia where everyone publishes and reviews content.

Another model of collaborative sites refers to site link aggregators, or "social bookmarking," where each member displays links to their favorite content so that others can use and vote for the best. In this way, a directory is created where the sites are recommended and classified by the participants themselves. So, if you want a website about wines, you can go to an aggregator and see the most recommended sites. One of the most famous in this category is Delicious, but Pinterest is also a kind of visual aggregator.

Collaboration in social media was also brought to the news, in a kind of collaborative journalism, so-called news aggregators like Reddit and Digg, are collected from users post themselves.

As a more personal approach, multimedia storage sites allow you to save your photos or videos and make them available to your friends, followers, or the entire Internet. They are a kind of world stage, where people promote themselves with the level of exposure that they want. YouTube in videos and Instagram in photos are some well-known and successful multimedia storage sites.

Social media is directly linked to the search tools, either internal to the platform itself or external, since its vast amount of content ends up prevailing in search engines such as Google.

As the consumer used to look for information, using keywords, in search engines content within a website or social media is the first and most important form of communication with an online consumer.

The fact is that a vast number of Internet users begin browsing through some search engine. Even when you advertise on search engines through sponsored links, only a small percentage of this users will be hit by your ad. Thus, there remains a massive contingent of consumers who browse based on the content of social media, not based on advertising, regardless of its format.

There is an enormous audience who are looking for information, some of it associated with your business, and therefore potential customers.

To bring this audience, that is looking for information related to your market, into your business you should use the step of talking about your business to the connected consumer, gathering actions related to content, social media and search tools.

It's critical that you plan, create, and publish content on your website, app, or social media to make it more visible on the Internet and more appealing to the consumer.

Think about how you navigate when looking for something new. You go for example to Google, type in one or two keywords related to your search, such as "Mediterranean cruise," then you review the summary list that Google displays on the screen. This list contains a title, which is what you read first, and two lines of description. If you find something useful, you click on the title link. If not, you type in a different search term, maybe something more specific like "cruise vacation in the Mediterranean," and start again.

Every time you click on a headline, Google sends you to the corresponding website. You look at the site and if you do not find anything of interest you click the Back button on your browser and go back to your search. It is as simple as that. You search, analyze and refine the search and end up by adding to your favorites a selection of sites that you feel are relevant.

With most searches, you come across information, comparisons or offers relating to your search topic. But sometimes you find yourself on a blog or site with a multitude of interesting, relevant information.

In this case, you will be driven to add this site to your favorites or subscribe to the site's newsletter for more information. Moreover, it is highly likely that the next time you are looking for something on this topic, you will go straight to that site before you even search on Google.

For example, if you search for "Mediterranean holiday cruise", and find a site with information on cruises in the Mediterranean, and also about cruising in various parts of the world, there's a good chance you will save this site in your favorites and refer to it again in the future when you are ready to book another cruise.

Search engines are one of the primary channels for bringing new customers to your site. Sites, such as Google check your site content and display it to new customers when they are looking for something related to your business. If you do not have content related to these searches, customers will not find your site. And if you do not have content that is relevant, they will not stay once they get there.

This also happens with social media. When you publish relevant content on YouTube, Instagram, Slideshare, and the like, you expose your content to the social media and regular search engines, and to potential customers.

So, in short, if your site or social media, does not contain relevant content for customers who are making their purchasing decisions, they will find what they are looking for with one of your competitors.

So, talk about your business is the first digital marketing step, used as a tool for attracting new customers and for keeping them coming back.

This also requires various techniques and actions, from effective site design, optimization for search engines (SEO), social media posting, blogging, and many other activities for your business to be visible on Google and social media search engines, and ensuring it is appealing to your customers.

Talk about your business also means focus on actions that generate results that are proportional to the investment. There is no point investing in professional SEO (search engine optimization) for your company website if it is only five pages long and contains little content of interest to your customers.

There is no sense of having a profile on YouTube if you don't have a plan on how to produce and post videos.

The key here is to position itself well in searches and create relevant customer-focused content.

In the following pages, we will take a look at the top strategies your business must employ at this first step.

## DEFINE YOUR TARGET AUDIENCE, CLEARLY AND SPECIFICALLY

Never begin any marketing activity without a specific target audience in mind. Your ideal customer is one who both needs and values your product or service. What is his profile?

Your ideal customer should already be defined in your business plan, but the truth is that many business owners have never thought objectively about this. If you have not already established your target market, this is an excellent opportunity to do so.

Describe your ideal client - his income, geographical location, age range, education, habits, behavior and other criteria that typify your customers.

Think primarily about whom your target market is online. If necessary, do some research - talk to customers, find discussion groups on the Internet, meet with colleagues and use every source of information you have at your disposal.

A word of warning: Do not work on false premises by assuming that a particular group is not very Internet-savvy or that as a business owner you know your customers. You will probably be surprised.

Many businesses have several target audiences, but you do not need to deal with all of them online. Consider who uses the Internet the most, who runs the most Google searches and social media and who therefore is most likely to be influenced by your content publishing.

Define your audience in writing and keep this description to hand whenever you carry out any marketing activities or meetings to ensure that your actions remain focused.

## PLAN YOUR CONTENT

Plan what content you can produce and publish on your website or blog for your customers. Think about what your consumers look for on the Internet before making their purchasing decision. Do not focus on what content you like or on your company's products. Think about what content will actually attract your target audience.

Do not place your focus on your products or services, focus on creating useful information. Try and think as your customers feel when they are searching on Google, or browsing at the social media, for a product or service that is provided by a company like yours.

To talk about your company, you need to produce and publish content, and you can follow these steps when planning what to do:

1. Who is your target audience? You already answered this question, now include it explicitly in your plan.

2. What do you want from your audience? Do you want them to come across your company and go to one of your physical stores? Do you want them to buy online? Do you want them to get in touch by phone? Do you want to create a desire to purchase your product? Do you want them to think your product is fresh? Define what you want to do with your customers when they get to your content.

3. How does your target audience behave? You know who they are, now research how they act. Are they frequent online shoppers? Are they proactive and collaborative? Are they loyal to a particular brand or website? It is essential that you understand their behavior to decide what content you should present to them for their first contact.

4. What information is your target audience looking for? You cannot produce content for everyone and everything. Think about the essential information your

customers search for when making their decision to buy a product or service. Put yourself in their shoes. What do you do, or what would you do before deciding to buy in this market? Would you look for company recommendations, comments or references? What information does your customer look for before buying?

5. What content should you produce for your audience? You have defined what information they look for, now you need to identify what content you are going to deliver. Information and content are very different things. If you are looking for information about restaurants, you will find content such as restaurant descriptions, customer reviews, or experts' views. Decide what content you believe is most relevant to your customers and consider what you can produce.

6. How do you create this content? Now that you know what you need to produce plan how to produce it and where to publish it. Do not underestimate the importance of this step. You need to determine the time and resources necessary to create content and decide what platforms to publish it on. Even if you want to produce the content yourself, this takes time. Think about the reality of producing content week after week, month after month, year after year.

# ALLOCATE RESOURCES

This will not happen by magic. You will need to allocate the right resources to produce and publish your company's content. Think of this investment as really talking about your business to an audience that is actually searching for it on the Internet.

You might use an intern, an employee, a supplier or even do it yourself. But whoever you choose, make sure they have a set time on a set day of the week allocated to this activity.

Allocate sufficient resource to continue the planning, production, and publication of content on an ongoing basis.

A common problem with businesses is that a lack of resources can lead to a loss of focus. So, you need to allocate resources that can sustain the production, publication, and updating of content in both the short and the medium term.

It is all too common for companies to create great content strategies that successfully attract new customers, only to discontinue the effort because day-to-day issues get in the way. They have everything in place but cannot sustain the resource in the longer term. Remember: customers never stop looking for information, researching and buying. If you leave the game, your competitors will supply these clients instead.

## CREATE YOUR BLOG

We will assume here that you already have a website. And if you do not, you will be creating one after reading this book. But to produce, publish and update content you need a publishing tool.

In fact, you need a set of publishing tools as you need to produce content in different formats and media, like video, text, and images. You will use a blog for text content, Youtube for video content and Instagram for pictures, and you can expand this using other social media like Pinterest.

As a headquarters for your content, and the baseline for the talk step, you need to a blog within your site, and integrate the other social media on it. Something like:

http://www.yoursite.com/blog

Use practical tools that are free of charge such as WordPress (www.wordpress.org) for creating your blog and managing your content. Most website hosting suppliers have free installations of WordPress that can be easily incorporated into your current site.

Your blog can appear in the menu on your site and must have the same domain name (URL) - usually something like www.yoursite.com/blog. The published articles can also be incorporated into the main page of your site as news or information items.

If you do not have a website or are thinking of updating it, note that many businesses have used their own WordPress as a platform to create website pages and content at the same time. Today these tools have evolved so much that your site can be developed directly in them, merely choosing the layout that is most suitable for your business.

## PROMOTE

Continually promote your content; or rather advertise links to the new pages or articles posted on your site. Do not wait for people to find them. Help your content to gain a profile in social media, blogs, Twitter, Facebook, and LinkedIn.

Integrate your blog with Twitter, so that every time you post content, it is displayed to your followers on Twitter. If you use WordPress, there is a Plugin that performs precisely this function.

Make the most of every opportunity to share your content. Add information to your email signature. Participate in forums and discussion groups. Read blogs related to your business and comment on articles using your signature.

Never miss an opportunity, especially in the early days of content publishing. Over time, some blogs may ask to reproduce your content. Give permission, with the proviso that they cite its source, in this case by including a link back to the original article on your site.

## FOCUS IS EVERYTHING

Stay focused and do not be tempted by mixing advertising into your content or creating untargeted texts. It is very common for companies to want to publish articles about their products and you can dedicate an area on your site just to this. But use your content to provide customers with the information they are trying to find.

Focus on content that is relevant to your customer community, being sure to keep it up to date and useful to your audience.

Make sure the content you post is targeted at the same customers that your site aims to sell to. If it is, sales will follow as a natural progression.

## MONITOR THE RESULTS

This initial effort will pay off, and it will not be long before customers searching on the Internet will find your content and make contact with your company.

It is critical that your site has a contact page to make life easy for your customers. WordPress has Plugins that can provide this function. This contact page is also useful for helping you to gauge interest and gather feedback from your customers on the content you produce.

Periodically check which items are most read, group them and determine what issues are most relevant to your customers. Invest more resources in these areas. Monitoring which pages and content are most read will help you understand what interests your target audience and improve your content planning.

If there is a spike in visits to a particular article, investigate why. Often a subject published in the mass media can help increase visits to your site. If the press releases a story about something related to your business, online audiences tend to do further research on Google about the theme. Publishing an article about it will help you tap into this new audience.

Also, check out which articles keep readers on your site longer and which lead them to visit the other pages on your site. You may find that while a particular post may not be the most popular, it attracts attention from customers who really intend to make a purchase. In the same way, you may notice that a particular type of article delivers more customers to the rest of the site.

The rule here is simple – monitor, monitor, monitor and learn. And never forget that the purpose of digital marketing is to get results.

## NEXT STEP

You learned the first step, talk about your business, producing relevant content, in the format of texts, images, podcasts, and videos, and then publish them in social media, and make them accessible to searches. The focus of the first step is on Content, Social Media and Search tools.

Next, we will show the second step, interact with your customers and the influencers.

# STEP 2 - INTERACT

## WORKING ON SOCIAL NETWORKS

Once you already know what to talk to the consumer about, the second step is to interact with him and the influencers who already talk to your consumer. And interacting implies talking, listening and sharing, it is an ongoing process that requires attention and above all skilled and trained human resources. It's like the shop attendant. It's no use putting up a nice store, with shelves full of useful products, if you employ poorly trained salespeople. They will ruin your store.

And in the digital ecosystem, the primary vehicle where you have the opportunity to focus your efforts on interacting with consumers and influencers are social networks. They are all kind of websites and applications where people register, build a profile and develop a relationship with other people, posting photos, sending messages, and creating groups or lists of friends. Throughout the world, a large part of the population participates in some social network, so they must be understood and considered in any business activity. Among the leading social networks are Facebook, LinkedIn, and Twitter.

An essential feature of social networking is its constant connection with users' daily lives. The large volume of people interacting, and the ability to aggregate and share content, especially from the intensive use of smartphones, makes consumers regularly communicate through social networks. This implies that even if you do not have any activity in there, there is a considerable probability that your consumers will use the social networks to talk about their experiences with your products, services or your brand.

So even if you do not post anything on social networks, it is critical that your digital identity includes profiles on key networks so you can interact with your consumers. However, this is not done without resources. In business, someone will have to devote a few hours a day interacting, and an average or large company will have to hire a person or a team to do so.

Finally, it should be emphasized that nowadays interacting is not restricted to social networks. Customer service has transformed, and most consumers expect your business to be able to serve yourself online and interactively. Since then, many tools have emerged for online service, through chat tools, support, frequently asked questions (FAQ), or even virtual assistants.

Interact refers to the collection of digital marketing activities aimed at giving support and expand your customer base by building online relationships between the company and the consumer via social networks.

Interact involves communicating with your customers online, not advertise. One of the biggest mistake companies make when using social networks is trying to promote their products and services without creating relationships with their audience.

No one wants to be the party bore. You wouldn't walk into a party chanting your product name, shouting about your current offers or giving out leaflets. Social places are places for people to have fun and communicate with each other, not for advertising. Social networks platforms are social places, so do not do it here either. Use them to meet people, communicate with them and contribute. Later who knows, you may get the chance to carry out a promotion or some kind of commercial activity.

Content produced in the first step is a vital part of this process. It helps to maintain a more constant conversation, thereby facilitating the relationship and involvement.

Always think of social media as a place to bond with your customers. Focus on relationship strategies. If you maintain a relationship with people, sooner or later they will visit your site and, when they need them, they will seek your products and services.

Furthermore, if you have used social networks to develop a good relationship with your audience, they can later become excellent platforms for carrying out sales promotions, announcing new launches and serving your customers. But you need to develop those relationships first.

The social networks are a vast area, and the only thing limiting what you can use it for is creativity. You do need to start with some practical steps, however, to create strong relationship foundations and establish your company image.

In the following pages, we will take a look at the most essential steps you need to grasp within your business.

## USE YOUR BLOG

As we saw in the talk step, it is essential to create a blog on your company website and keep it up to date. This facilitates communication and keeps your customers informed.

The vast majority of social networks such as Twitter, Facebook, and LinkedIn offer tools for updating your profile posts from your blog. So, when you publish something new, your customers will be updated via their social networks.

Furthermore, this makes it much easier for them to share your content with other people there by liking it, re-tweeting it or sharing it

Note that people often focus just on one or two social networks. They may read blogs only occasionally and use email sparingly. So, set up your social network profiles and use the articles from your blogs to feed them, and you will increase the exposure of your business.

The content you produce is an excellent way to start a social network conversation. It is readily accepted, useful for those who are connected to you and often helpful to share with your customers' friends.

## CREATE YOUR TWITTER PROFILE

Twitter has expanded rapidly as an information center and is now used by your customers, by journalists, by bloggers, and by influencers in your market. It must, therefore, be one of the basics of your interact strategy.

Create a profile for yourself, your company or your blog on Twitter. Search for people who are essential to your business and start following them.

Install an application on your blog to tweet your articles (as I mentioned earlier WordPress already offers this as a plugin) and complement it by writing once a day about exciting things that happen with your business.

Twitter is an essential tool for viral campaigns and promotions. But leave these until you have a stable follower base. Viral campaigns and promotions work best once people have an established relationship with you.

## MAKE A MAP

Make a map of influencers on your market, listing the leading blogs and social media profiles, that discuss topics that are related to your business and that your customers may also be reading. This is very useful for all digital marketing activities.

Your list should contain at least fifteen blogs and social media profiles related to your business. Find them by searching on Google, Facebook, Youtube, Twitter, and

Instagram for related themes and looking at which one are most active and appear most frequently in the search results.

Subscribe to the respective feeds or channels and follow them once a week.

Leave comments whenever you see an interesting post on one of these influencers, adding your email and your website address in the comment signature when possible. This will help raise the profile of your company.

Over time you will make connections with the influencers, and you will be able to have your links or articles published by them.

Another advantage of this relationship is that you can feed your social networks with links to articles of these influencers. Whenever you see something of interest to your audience, you can share the link on your social networks.

Your relationship with influencers can also help with sales promotions and launches. If you have launched a new product, invite influencers you know to try it out. Some of them may request samples or products to use as prize draws for their followers, which also increases their exposure.

## CREATE YOUR PROFILE IN NETWORKS

Which social networks should your company join? If you try to get involved with the hundreds of new social networks that pop up each month, you will probably make a lot of bad bets and invest resources in platforms that give you no return.

As a business, your digital marketing should be focused. And your focus is simple: You have to be where your customer is.

You cannot be everywhere, so consider which social networks are most relevant to your customers. If necessary, talk to some of your customers and find out what they use: Facebook, Twitter, LinkedIn, Etsy? It is your customers who will dictate which social networks you use.

In some cases, you may be surprised and find that they use a niche network such as Etsy, a platform focused on arts and crafts.

Create a profile for you, your company or your blog on the most relevant social networks. Look for forums, communities and interest groups and join them. Keep track of your contacts and messages almost every day. Smartphones notifications are great for this job.

Above all, keep control of your resources and your time. It is better to have a presence in two social networks and really relate to their members than to create dozens of profiles on multiple social networks and be unable to maintain those relationships.

Remember that when you put a company profile on a social network, your customers will feel at right to write, ask questions and request support through that network. And there is nothing more frustrating than a company profile that gives you no response.

Create a professional profile on LinkedIn for yourself, rather than for your company, and do the same for any other professional network that is appropriate to you. Do the first networking on LinkedIn by including former work and study colleagues and join groups that interest you.

Keep track of your contacts and messages once a week.

## GO BEYOND THE PROFILES

You will often need to go beyond creating profiles and exchanging information with your customers. Many social networks allow for the creation of theme-based discussion groups, and it is essential to participate in those that are of most interest to your company.

You can take this even further by creating a group based on a subject that linked to your company and leading it. This doesn't work well for all businesses, but if you dominate a theme that is related directly to your business, it can be an excellent way of grouping customers and influencers around your company.

## DO NOT SPAM

Never use social networks for sending mass messages and resist the temptation to advertise openly in your posts.

Remember that you can be blocked from any social network and sending mass advertising is the quickest way to destroy your customer relationships.

It is much more effective just to include your name, e-mail, and website as a standard signature on any post you make.

Social networks are not like conventional media. This isn't television, radio or a newspaper, where an advertisement is a familiar place. If you want to advertise, use the space and tools that are designed for online advertising in that social network. Never advertise via your social network profile or that of your company. We will talk about online advertising later in this book.

## INTERACT WITH YOUR CUSTOMERS

Increasingly, customers want to be served by companies via the same channels as they interact with them.

If you use Twitter for a promotion, be prepared to deal with questions, complaints, and suggestions via Twitter. If you have a Facebook profile, stay logged in, because your customers will use this same channel to ask questions and interact with your company.

Follow this golden rule for social networks: Listen first, interact when necessary and respond when asked.

If a consumer makes a complaint via a social network, resolve it and then communicate the solution. And do it fast. The potential for generating goodwill by dealing with your customers effectively via a social network is higher than you think.

When you are dealing with clients on your social networks to resolve a problem, or when you receive criticism through them, remember that customers are not looking for perfect companies, just companies that care about them.

## PROMOTIONAL ACTIVITY

Once you are confident you have a good network of relationships in social media, it is time to use them for some promotional activity.

Start by creating simple promotions that are easy to understand and have clear rules.

Consider what you will offer. Perhaps a product discount, a prize draw or competition and decide the entry rules. Consider whether the offer will make sense to your customers and if anything can go wrong. Think too about what will happen if it goes very well.

Many social networks promotions go wrong because companies do not scope out the project well enough. For example, the campaign may be successful, but there may be a shortage of product to supply all the customers. This is not always the case, but be entirely sure you can deliver what is promised.

If you can only supply ten customers, ensure you make this clear. If you can just deliver to a particular region, say so. Only promise what you can definitely deliver.

Running sales promotions on social networks is also a great way of controlling your stock and selling products that have been stuck on the shelves.

You need to start with simple promotions and expand your offers as you gain more confidence on it.

## BE FOCUSED AND KEEP THE CONVERSATION FLOWING

Set aside some time once a week to work your customer relationships on social networks. Here again, we come back to the need to plan your resources for the short and medium term. The most important thing is to create something that is constant.

## NEXT STEP

You learned the second step, interact with your customers via social networks, create a map to interact with influencers, sharing the content you produced at the first step, and attending your customers via the same channel. The focus of the second step is two-way communication via social networks.

Next, we will show the third step, tell the news to your existing customers.

# STEP 3 - TELL

## CREATING A DIRECT RELATIONSHIP

When you talk and interact, you end up engaging a group of people to your brand, which you have more direct and unique access to, usually through a previous registration, either through email, WhatsApp, or other direct communication apps. To maintain the relationship with this group of consumers to whom we have direct access you have to go further and tell them about your activities, your business, your market and any type and theme that may interest a closer consumer.

A long time ago, the priority communication vehicle for this direct marketing was the e-mail, which emerged as a form of communication already in the early days of the Internet. The e-mail quickly replaced many other types of personal and business communication and for a long time was the identity of the people on the network.

However, generation Z and millennium, which are made up of young people born after 1987, use instant messaging, such as WhatsApp, Messenger, and Skype. Also, e-mail suffers a lot with the so-called spam, the sending of unsolicited messages, and with the viruses and scams sent by that means. After all, e-mails remain a popular form of communication on the Internet.

Companies to develop direct marketing adapted the old traditional mailing to email and created the so-called email marketing. This tool has grown a lot and becoming diversified with new graphics solutions, trying to ensure that the message actually reaches the consumer. Like all direct mail, the result was low compared to the volume of emails sent, creating the need to address an increasing amount of emails for satisfactory results.

Here is essential to differentiate email marketing from spam, which is not always easy, especially if you have purchased an email list that is not yours but from another company. It is also difficult to ensure that your email marketing is not confused with viruses or scams.

However, telling is not just email marketing or newsletters. First, you need to develop a timeline where each message that is sent makes sense and has a purpose, then it is necessary to include all current direct communications, and allow the consumer to decide in which channel to receive messages.

Here is an important consideration. The technology evolves very quickly, so we mean that we are using the word communication channel in the broadest possible sense, including e-mail and any type of individualized message delivery medium, but can be sent in bulk to specific recipients. This includes emails, WhatsApp, notifications, SMS, and any other type of communication medium that exists to send a direct message to the consumer.

Email marketing is a form of digital marketing, and while it is perhaps the most popular digital marketing tool for businesses, it is almost certainly the most misused digital marketing tool across the world.

Thus, we can say that if you only present brief information at the end of your email, it's a mistake since your audience may not be patient enough to read through. Therefore, from the start, tell your viewers your main point, so that they can make decisions much quicker.

Email marketing is mainly direct marketing, aimed at establishing direct contact with customers and passing them a message.

But direct marketing and email marketing suffer from an embarrassing level of SPAM emails and scams. Furthermore, many companies use it to send advertising indiscriminately to a massive number of people who are mostly, if not all, of no use.

Think of the number of useless e-mails you receive and plan your email marketing to avoid your customers having the same experience with your company.

The challenge of email marketing is to use it as a differentiator and to make its useful to their customers. The aim is to get your customers to follow the following steps:

1. Do not delete your email.

2. Do not mark your email as spam.

3. Read the subject line of your email and have their interest aroused.

4. Open your email and read its contents.

5. Remain interested in learning other emails you send.

To achieve this, follow my golden rule of email marketing:

Send useful information. Send it to the right people. And make sure they actually want to receive it.

In practice, you need to create a basic scenario to ensure your email marketing is relevant to your consumer. In the following pages, we will focus on the actions you need to take in your business to achieve this scenario.

## CREATE A USEFUL AND EFFICIENT LIST

Create and maintain your own database for your email marketing. The most important thing is to send messages to the right people and to know that they will open and read your message.

Purchasing lists of companies can be a waste of time and money. Think about how many times have you received messages from companies that do not fit your profile, and with whom you will never do business.

Remember: only buy email lists from companies that clearly state how the emails were obtained. Pirated or unqualified lists will be made up of customers who do not want to receive your emails. If lists are unqualified, it means that someone at some point is using the customer's address without his authorization. This is wrong and can be harmful to your business.

Furthermore, people selling pirated or unqualified lists are selling to thousands of people and companies indiscriminately. This means in practice that the poor souls who appear in these lists receive thousands of spam emails and are therefore less likely to read your email.

## CREATE EMAILS WITH GOOD CONTENT

Do not send an entire brochure in your communication campaign, nor a message that just contains images. The recipient's email client blocks the image, and he can't see anything, thus reducing the chances of him persevering.

Mix images and texts in a way that even if the reader's email client blocks the images, he can still read the text and understand the message.

Format your message so that it is easy to read and understand. Create a template and use this as standard in all your messages so your customers can identify with your message.

Also, pay attention to the subject line of your email. Aim to write something that catches the attention of the reader and clearly identifies your company. Remember, the email subject is the first thing the reader sees. Make sure it is attractive and appropriate for your business.

## SET AN AGENDA

When planning your email marketing think of the best timing for your customers. When will they be most likely to open and read your message?

Different groups of people tend to have different patterns of email use. For example, office-based executives have a lot of SPAM (unwanted emails) waiting for them on Monday mornings because they often do not read the email over the weekend. So, it is better to send emails to these groups on Tuesday or Wednesday afternoons.

On the other hand, university students may have little time during the week, making it more appropriate to send emails during the weekend.

So, it is vital that you identify the best day of the week or month and the best time to send emails to your target audience.

Establish the best time and day and back this up with some tests, by emailing contacts on your list on different days and times and analyzing which give the best results.

## HAVE A REGISTRATION FORM

Many people visit your site and social networks, or at least they should, so do not let them escape. Create a page on your website where they can register for email marketing.

Create opportunities for registration at all points of contact with your customers, such as in your store, with your salespeople, in your business card or on registration forms.

Your existing customers and those who make contact with your company are your starting point for all email marketing activities.

## CREATE CAMPAIGNS

An excellent way to increase the attention your customers pay to the emails your company sends them is by creating promotional campaigns that are unique to email.

Periodic campaigns, promotions and exclusive discounts keep your customers interested in your emails and make them pay more attention to messages sent by your company.

In these campaigns, make it clear that the discount or offer is only valid via the link sent in the email and stick to it. Even if you run a seasonal promotion, for instance at Christmas, why not give an additional discount of 5% or 10% solely to those who click on the link sent in the email promotion.

Make your customers understand that there is a unique advantage to being registered on your mailing list.

## CREATE RECOMMENDATION CAMPAIGNS

The most efficient way to expand your mailings is through the recommendations of people who already read them. If I have a customer who reads my email and likes my brand, it is likely that he knows other people who might like it too.

So, allow and encourage your customers to recommend new people to sign up to your email list.

Periodically create "Refer a Friend" campaigns and promotions for new registrations. Offer a short-term incentive such as a prize for the person who refers the most friends in a month or for a longer-term motivation use a points system with rewards for people who achieve a certain number of referrals

## TALK TO YOUR CUSTOMERS

Sending brochures by email is the easiest way of losing your customers. Do not carry advertising, do the opposite - tell them about you.

Create a weekly newsletter with updates on your business. If your company does not generate much news, including information about your industry that your customers will find interesting.

You can use your blog content for this. Select the best articles and send a newsletter with short summaries and links to the complete articles.

It is better to keep your customers well informed by email, getting them used to opening and reading your newsletters every two weeks than to send advertising. Once people get used to reading useful information in your newsletter, you can start to include a section with products and new launches.

## DO NOT BE A BORING

The worst propaganda is boring propaganda. Do not send millions of emails, do not post image brochures and do not just talk about your products.

Consider why someone would open what you are sending and whether it is actually relevant to your customers.

I enjoy receiving information about tourist destinations before the school holidays, but I delete everything I receive on this subject during the rest of the year. You probably got the idea. When you are sending email marketing, only send interesting messages and genuine and exclusive offers.

## NEXT STEP

You learned the third step, tell the news to your existing customers via direct communication channels, not only e-mail but also WhatsApp, Messenger, SMS and the like. Follow the communication rules we present at this step and remember the golden rule of telling is: Send useful information. Send to the right people. And make sure they actually wish to receive it.

Next, we will show the fourth step, push your message to the digital media and increase your audience.

# STEP 4 - PUSH

## EXPAND YOUR AUDIENCE

Nevertheless, strategies for talking, interacting and telling span a known group of close customers, which in most businesses are not enough to support them, either because they are small or because the company is meant to expand continuously to survive. Of course, these three steps extend their target audience over time as consumers share their content, their interactions, or their direct messages, attracting new consumers.

So the first three steps, talk, interact and tell, are focused on keep and expand your customer base constantly over time. But to grow your customer base faster, and at an appropriate pace, you need to take other actions that push and spread your message. The fours step is about the push, and the fifth step is about the spread.

Push means broadening your target audience using other digital media beyond your current audience, which are all potential consumers who still have little or no contact with your brand through your website, social media, social networks, or your direct mail. For this we have to use paid media and publishing advertising pieces that attract the attention of this consumer, pushing our brand beyond its current border.

Historically, online advertising started with banners published on websites, copying the model of the ads served in the outdoor and printed media. With time and new technologies, however, the banners have gained interaction, sound, video, animation, and many other features. Also, new alternatives have emerged, such as widgets, podcast, videocast, and game marketing, and tools like Google AdWords have been running interactive banners. Over time almost all media, social media and social networks have started to have online advertising tools, including Facebook and Youtube.

Today the online advertising alternatives are diverse, and technologies that can be employed as well. The most important thing is to understand that it is a different model of the advertising model on television, radio, print or outdoor media, and copying pieces of such media to online advertising may not be the best alternative. Also, the purpose of online advertising must be to push your brand, your business, and your products to an expanded online consumer group.

Push means the collection of digital marketing activities aimed at promoting your brand or product within paid media. While it may appear similar to conventional advertising, online media differs in several ways from traditional media, and online advertising has its own unique characteristics.

Before you invest your money by placing banner ads or sponsored links, it is essential that you understand what it is:

1. It is multimedia: The online advertising environment involves various media and technologies, offering you several alternatives such as text, banners, interactive banners, podcasts, videos, widgets, and online games.

2. It is distributed through many channels: Each website, portal, social media or social network has its own distribution and ads mechanism. On top of that, there are different payment methods such as pay-per-click where you pay for each visitor sent to your site, pay-per-view where you pay for each time your ad is seen, or space rotation where you pay a monthly fee to run your ad.

3. It is dispersed: The online media audience is very dispersed, and the audience is not always well established or easy to identify. Unlike a magazine or radio show which has a clear audience, it is much harder to determine the exact profile of a website, portal or social network audience on the Internet.

So businesses need to familiarize themselves with all the different ways to push the message via online advertising to determine which is the most relevant to them. In the following pages, we will explore these alternatives further to help you identify which is the best for your business.

## START WITH RESEARCH

Digital media is highly fragmented. Focus on vehicles such as sites that are explicitly targeted at your customers, like blogs that discuss issues that are of interest to them. This keeps your costs down and provides greater certainty of your advertisement is seen by the right target audience.

To choose these websites and blogs, create a list of sites that are relevant to your business. Do this by using the same search tools that your customers use when looking for these sites for the first time.

We will cover this in more detail in the sixth step: Online research. But the important thing here is that you keep an up-to-date list of the most relevant online media to carry your business's online advertising.

## USE BANNERS

Banners are a good option for any company. Hire a professional to create an animated or interactive banner for your business.

Unless you are an advertising agency, do not try to make your own banners. If you do some research, you will find plenty of professionals who can create great banners for you within your budget.

Create something different that really catches attention. Avoid creating a standard banner and try to create a piece that will attract your customers and lead them to interact with your brand.

Produce these banners in all the formats you could need.

Reserve a portion of your monthly budget that you feel is appropriate and use it to publish this banner.

You can publish your banner directly on the sites contained in your list through the Google AdWords content network. You can also release them via your preferred social network, using Facebook, Twiter, Instagram advertising tools.

## USE VIDEOS

Videos are a powerful tool for online advertising and can act as a kind of own television show for your company. Start by creating an account and a channel for your company on YouTube and set the channel layout to reflect your business's identity.

Then create videos about your business. Do not think about advertising your products, just focusing on making videos that reflect and meet your customers' interests concerning your business.

Post these videos on your YouTube channel and track the results. Play videos on your site or blog using YouTube's tools and publicize links to them in your social networks.

Focus on educating, entertaining or amusing your audience. You can create an educational series, explanatory videos for using your products and informative videos on topics that are related to your business and your customers' interests. Look at videos made by companies similar to yours and use them as inspiration for making your own.

You can also use a part of these videos, like an online preview advertising in media that support them, to attract customers to your video channel.

## THINK ABOUT ONLINE GAMES

Online games are on the rise. If your target audience includes youngsters, invest in the creation of an excellent online game. Again, do your research and hire the right professional within your budget.

You can run your game on your website and thus attract new consumers, or you can harness the viral effect of Internet games. Produce your game as a widget (small application) that can be installed on other websites and blogs so that bloggers and influencers who like your game can become spontaneous promoters of your brand.

The game content should be related to your business and somehow achieve visibility for your brand. A good example would be to produce a pizza-making game for a network of pizzerias, or a shooting game for a network of paintball centers.

An attractive option for many businesses is the creation of games and applications for Facebook. This major social network has a platform that allows you to create apps and games that run on your site but which are integrated into your customers' Facebook profiles and can be run from within their accounts. Besides taking advantage of your customers' friend networks, Facebook applications and games offer several tools that facilitate viral growth.

# CARRY OUT SPONSORED LINK CAMPAIGNS

The sponsored link concept just keeps on growing. Where once they were exclusive to the search engines like Yahoo and Google, they have now expanded to appear in social networks like Facebook, Twitter, and LinkedIn as sponsored posts.

Sponsored links and posts are pay-per-click text advertisements run on search engines or social networks, that appear in specific locations during the customer's navigation process.

The big advantage is that sponsored links and posts are easy to create, available to businesses of all sizes and may have a reduced overall cost. Sponsored link and posts campaigns are better suited to some types of business than others, as depending on your audience and your kind of business these campaigns may yield much higher results than expected while in other cases, they prove not to be worth the investment. You will need to try them out to find out what kind of return to expect on your investment.

Create and publish sponsored link campaigns on Google, Facebook, Twiter, and LinkedIn. The idea is to start with a small monthly spend, running tests and making adjustments every month while measuring the overall result of each campaign. Over time you will discover what campaign format works best and which sites are most profitable for your business.

## SPONSORED LINK CAMPAIGNS TIPS

Sponsored links are paid advertisements that appear next to the search results when consumers search with specific keywords. They enable you to advertise to consumers who use search terms that are directly related to your product.

Social networks like Facebook and LinkedIn have also created sponsored link solutions, but instead of showing ads next to a user's search results they are displayed directly sponsored posts in the user profile. They still present according to specific keywords, but advertisers have more control over aspects of their audience profile such as age, education and other criteria.

Bear in mind that according to Google published data, less than 10% of searches generate a click on a sponsored link. The remaining 90% of the clicks are made directly on natural search results.

Another critical factor to consider is that not all clicks and visits originate from your target audience. People may misinterpret your ad, or they may click out of curiosity or for some other reason that is unrelated to your business, and these people will never become clients.

Sponsored link campaigns are useful and easy to implement, but you need to take care not to waste your advertising budget.

## DEFINE THE PURPOSE OF CAMPAIGN

Do not carry out general sponsored link campaigns. Each campaign should have a specific goal that is linked to your marketing needs.

Create a particular objective, linked to a campaign, promotion or launch.

Define the result you want to achieve and calculate how much you feel is worth investing in the campaign to make it. Start by setting a monthly budget that will be allocated throughout the year. It does not matter how big it is, it can be pretty small, but the important thing is that it is fixed, so you do not overspend.

Do not aim to sell everything at once, just focus on a specific goal with each campaign.

## CREATE THE BASIC KEYWORDS FOR YOUR CAMPAIGN.

With the information, you already put together in the first step, regarding relevant content, define a list of keywords for the campaign so that you can determine how you will achieve your objective.

Put yourself in the shoes of a customer searching for your products and consider how to reach them with your campaign. If necessary, test these keywords on search engines and see if the results are actually relevant to your business and your target audience.

The important thing is to think like your customers and try to understand in which moment he becomes interested in your business and products and match this with your campaign objective. Then consider how they will use search tools to satisfy their needs.

## RESEARCH THE KEYWORD TOOL

Each basic keyword acts as a guide to help you draw up a keyword list for each campaign. These ad group lists are the information that Google requires when you want to display the ad.

So, if you have a basic keyword like "chocolate," you can have a list of keywords such as "milk chocolate," "chocolate with raisins" and "chocolate sauce." Each time a consumer searches with a mix these words your ad will appear.

It is better to create ten advertisements each with twenty keywords, than one ad with hundreds of keywords.

To help create the keyword list from basic keywords, Google has a "Keyword Tool" (just type the term into Google search to find it), which helps by giving ideas about which terms should be used and what search volumes each one has.

## CREATE CAMPAIGN ADS

Create one or more ads directly linked to each list of keywords. Consider what your objectives are for each ad and be as specific as possible.

The ads have to call customers to action and offer something concrete to make them click on them, while at the same time your message must be clear to avoid clicks from people who are not interested in your offer.

Check out the terms of use for each sponsored link tool. Generally, some ad formats, such as using capital letters or phrases such as "click here" are prohibited by the terms of use.

## CREATE LANDING PAGES

Each ad should lead the customer to a dedicated campaign page and make a call for immediate action. These are called "landing pages." You must create one for each ad.

Never run ads that lead to your website home page as this reduces your campaign's effectiveness and lowers conversion rates.

The landing page should contain information that is directly related to your ad and use the keywords from your list in its text.

It should also contain some form of action or conversion so you can measure the effectiveness of the ad and the campaign. If you are selling your product or service online, place a purchase option directly on this page. If you are selling it through a physical store, tell your customers exactly where they can buy it and include a contact telephone number.

Another alternative is to create free gifts for your customers to download such as a how-to guide, an information chart, an image, or a promotional code. This makes it easier to analyze your results and measure your customers' intention to purchase.

## CREATE, PUBLISH AND MONITOR YOUR CAMPAIGN

With your ads and keyword lists prepared, you are ready to create your sponsored link campaign.

Create your campaign, set your daily budget, and send your campaign live. It is essential to monitor your campaign consistently. Never leave it live without analyzing its results on a weekly basis and making any necessary adjustments.

Check the results every day to start with and then move on to weekly analysis. Every sponsored link campaign needs tweaking. If you see over time that an ad is not delivering useful results, discontinue it and invest more in those that are.

Weekly campaign analysis not only optimizes your investment but it also helps you better understand your customers' search behavior, which can be useful across your entire digital marketing strategy.

## NEXT STEP

You learned the fourth step, push your message to the digital media and increase your audience, through online advertising, and sponsored links and posts. Remember to think like your customers, and check all the tips we present at this step.

Next, we will show the fifth step, to spread your message virally.

# STEP 5 - SPREAD

## VIRALIZE YOUR MESSAGE

The fifth step, to spread your message, will also help to expand your customer base. If in the fourth step, you push your message buying an audience from another media, what we call advertising, by spreading you will use your own audience, to spread your message through the so-called viral effect.

One of the main strengths of the Internet is the communication between one online user and another, the so-called word-of-mouth. As communications on the Internet are very fast and social networks, create massive networks of relationships, the effect of word of mouth is enhanced. On the Internet, this effect of spreading a message through word of mouth, by sending a message from one person to another, creates a chain reaction that spreads communication by thousands or millions of people without much effort. This is called a viral effect because it resembles what happens to a virus outbreak.

Thus, to spread your message means to use this effect to convey a marketing message and although it is based on one of the strengths of the Internet, the relationship, it can still be used by companies.

Creating a viral campaign to spread your message requires creativity and an understanding of the human being and his basic needs. Perhaps that is why only a few brands use these step. But you can not ignore this tool, which raises word-of-mouth to a level never seen before.

As it is often said, the best advertisement is word-of-mouth. So you need to know that it is possible to do it on the Internet in an agile and very efficient way. You need to understand that this is a great force of the digital ecosystem and that many brands and companies are being built or harmed by the viral effect of online communication. Think about this.

An online viral effect is a powerful tool, enabling you to spread your message to a significant number of people via the Internet.

In the online viral effect, you start by sending your message to a group of people, known as alpha users, who are motivated to share this message to others. If on average each person shares the message to two or more people, this creates a viral effect, and soon the message reaches thousands or even millions.

Let me give an example. If in an initial group of 100 people, each one passes the message to two others the next day, and they do the same in turn, within a week the message will have reached more than 12,000 people. But what is even more powerful is that if the viral effect continues, within a month the message will have reached more than 50 million people. This is the viral effect.

The viral effect has always existed. Every business benefits from word of mouth referrals by current clients to new customers. But the Internet has increased coverage and speed exponentially, transforming the viral effect into a viable marketing tool.

Almost all the big Internet successes, from Hotmail to WhatsApp, have benefited from the viral effect. But you can also create viral campaigns specifically to drive your business growth.

Viral marketing involves creativity and a good knowledge of your customers' values and behavior. The viral coverage that is generated creates exposure for your brand and businesses, and this can be a powerful Internet tool for creating competitive advantage.

But to create a significant viral effect, we must first understand the three main motivations that produce the viral effect:

> 1. Functional motivation: Here, the use of a product leads to the viral effect, such as with Hotmail and Dropbox. Each person who uses these services spreads the word to other users. In Hotmail, every email footer carries the advice that Hotmail is free and anyone can join. In Dropbox, you drop your documents into the cloud and send links to other users who register to access a document. The functional approach is particularly suitable for promoting new web services and software where you can embed the viral effect into the product.

2. Personal motivation: Here, it is someone's immediate personal interest motivates them, such as with affiliate programs like Amazon, where bloggers add banners to their blog's online store to win a share of sales. As well as promoting the company to their readers, other bloggers see this kind of banner and add it to their own blogs.

3. Emotional motivation: Here, intense emotion, whether positive or negative, is the motivator. This is the case with VW Fun Theory, the viral campaign in which the German manufacturer aims to create fun projects to motivate people to adopt sustainable attitudes. Another example is the successful YouTube video series "Will It Blend It?" in which a blender manufacturer challenges viewers to prove that their product is capable of blending anything, from golf balls to iPhones.

So, whenever you create a viral campaign, you need to define which of these motivators will be the driver. A typical promotional campaign on a social network, such as a prize draw, does not generate a viral effect. But an action where the winner is the person who produces the most visitors or registrations to the product website uses strong personal motivation, which creates a viral effect.

Viral marketing is an essential tool for business growth on the Internet, and you should aim to use it whenever possible. In the following pages, we take a look at the steps required to create a viral campaign for your business.

## UNDERSTAND YOUR CUSTOMERS AND LOOK FOR NICHES

A great place to get started with viral marketing is to select a niche market you want to reach but for which you have not yet created a clear communication strategy, or which you find it difficult to access.

Look at which social network is most used by the customers in this niche – this is the best place for your first viral marketing activity.

If you have difficulty identifying the right social network, just choose an established one like YouTube or Twitter.

Once you have chosen your niche and social media, you have the foundation to create a viral campaign.

When I launched my first book, I chose college students as my viral market niche. Students often have difficulty acquiring all the books they need and are not necessarily the primary consumers of an expensive book on digital marketing. But on the other hand, they have time and a willingness to promote things via social media, so I chose college students on Facebook as my niche group for launching my book.

## CREATE VIRAL MARKETING ACTIVITIES

Search on Google for three viral marketing campaigns for niches similar to the one you are targeting.

With your research material on hand, hold a brainstorming meeting (a meeting to generate ideas) with at least five people to come up with ideas for viral campaigns. If you do not have this kind of team or an agency at your disposal, invite customers, friends, and suppliers. If it is not practical to all meet together, share ideas via Skype or WhatsApp. But it is essential to talk with other people to get the ideas flowing.

Start by presenting your target niche and social network, and show the viral campaigns you collected in your research. Aim to leave this brainstorming session with at least one strong viral marketing campaign with your media defined (whether it be text, video, banner or audio) social network selected (Facebook, Twitter, YouTube), how you will begin the campaign, and who your starting group will be (what we call your alpha users).

Try to use a promotional text, video, or animated banner for your first viral piece, as these are easier to produce for the first time. Pay attention to details and quality.

Be creative and produce something you are proud of. If you want an immediate example of what I mean, look on YouTube for "Will It Blend It?"

In the example I gave about the release of my first book, after doing some research I decided that we should produce a promotional text inviting students to take part in a competition. Whoever spread the message and brought the most visitors to the book page by the end of one week would receive an autographed copy. All they needed to do was go to the promotion page on the website, create a custom link, and publish it on Facebook and Twitter. The site counted how many visits originated from each link, and at the end of the week, the student who brought the most hits won the autographed copy.

## PROMOTE THE VIRAL PIECE

Publish your viral marketing piece by placing it on your chosen social network, for example by uploading your video on YouTube, posting the link to the rules on Twitter, or something similar. This is known as seeding your viral piece.

Promote this piece to your alpha users and work with them. It is essential to inform a minimum starting group about the video or promotion, so they know about it.

Do not refer to it as a viral campaign when you communicate with this group, just post messages talking about the video or tweet about the promotion with a link to the rules.

And finally, follow up the campaign, especially at the beginning so that you are available to answer any questions or correct any errors. If the action has not been planned or developed well, doubts and criticism will surface immediately upon its release. You will need to be on the spot to correct any errors and make any changes you feel are necessary to improve the campaign and its viral effect.

When I launched my book, I just published an announcement about the contest on my Twitter and Facebook accounts. The text went something simple like this:

"Prove that you understand about Digital Marketing and win an autographed copy of The Digital Marketing Bible."

## LEARN FROM ALL THIS

Learn from your experience with spreading your message with own viral activities.

If the viral campaign fails to take off and generate a significant return, try to understand why so that you get the next one right.

If it is satisfactory, well done. Carry on.

If it is excellent, make a case study and share it to inspire others, as part of your talk effort at step 1.

Publishing a case study of a successful viral marketing campaign can itself create a viral effect. Journalists, advertisers, and students may be interested in hearing about it and publishing their own texts discussing it. This helps create yet more exposure for your business.

## NEXT STEP

You learned the fifth step, spread your message using the online viral effect, planning an impressive viral piece, and using alpha users. Remember to learn from each viral campaign and keep improving. You are building a competitive advantage, and it is worthwhile.

Next, we will show the sixth step, to search, to build knowledge as a competitive advantage.

# STEP 6 - SEARCH

## KNOWLEDGE AS A COMPETITIVE ADVANTAGE

At this point, you learn three steps to creating a steady growth by talking, telling and interacting with your existing consumers. You also learned two steps to grow beyond your current boundaries, by pushing and spreading your message online. But you also need a step to establish a competitive advantage by seeking constant knowledge about your online market, competitors, and consumers.

Search also means research and is the basis of any marketing activity. In the offline world, it is done by people, with a lot of effort and investment, but the Internet has the characteristics of a persistent media, that means everything that is written or published stays there. An example is Facebook, where each group is a discussion forum. The content that users post in the community forum is registered and can be consulted years later.

Because that is persistent, the Internet allows for more elaborate and cheaper searches than regular surveys, based on tests or interviews. Instead of asking people what they think, you can just read what they have already written about it.

Furthermore, the online search can be supported by computer programs, the so-called robots or "spiders." Robots are applications that run on servers and access websites on the Internet, capturing their content and storing it for later use. Many companies have "online clipping" services, that capture selected content, usually based on keywords, chosen by the client. Another online search aspect is the media search, where you get information about websites, social media, blogs and forums related to a particular subject.

The search step adds knowledge to your business about your consumers, your competitors, and your market, creating a competitive advantage for you.

The five steps we have seen so far, talk, interact, tell, push and spread, will help your business to become better known, better liked, more commented upon and seen by more consumers on the Internet. Each of these steps will help you to learn and grow your business.

But to be successful online and to make your business grow and increase sales, you also need a competitive advantage, and online search involves the use of existing information on the Internet to create digital intelligence for your company.

Your customers, the media and some of your competitors will have already been using the Internet for some time - writing, commenting, suggesting and discussing ideas, products, and services related to your industry. So online search is the step that aims to provide your business with competitive intelligence.

Carrying out search helps you to very quickly understand your customers and their needs, analyze what competitors are doing and understand their strengths and weaknesses, and see how the media and social networks are positively or negatively affecting your business.

All businesses should invest in online search and create strong digital competitive intelligence, and in the following pages, we will explore the online search you should use for your business.

## ASK QUESTIONS AND CARRY OUT RESEARCH

Define a set of at least three key questions for your business. A key question is one whose answer creates a competitive advantage for your business.

Consider something that would give you a competitive advantage if only you knew the answer. For instance, for a gourmet coffee business, a key question might be "What would convince a customer to choose a gourmet coffee, even if it was more expensive?"

Asking this question directly to your customers would not work. You could not guarantee an honest response, and in any case, it is not necessarily something that the customer considers at the exact moment of purchase.

Your key question will be put to far better use as the basis of some online search.

An online opinion poll online should not take the form of a questionnaire that you send to your customers. Instead, you should look to information that already exists in social media and social networks to answer your key question.

Spontaneous discussions in social network forums, groups and communities are all archived and their content searchable using their associated search engines. This should form the basis of your working material.

Follow these five steps to implement your online search program:

> 1. Choose your questions: Start with the questions that are most essential to your business. You can create new questions once you have completed your first survey.
>
> 2. Define your information sources: Which websites, forums, social networks or blogs could be useful sources of information for your research? Think broadly, but focus on social media that has the most significant volume of information on the subject.
>
> 3. Define your media format: You need to define what formats you will search and collect, i.e., whether you will collect texts, images, videos or multiple media formats.
>
> 4. Define your keywords: All social networks (YouTube, Flickr, Twitter, Facebook, Blogs and Forums) have their own search tools to help you find the information you need for your research. So transform your question into a list of keywords.

5. Implement your search: Go to the social networks, use the keywords, find conversations and discussions that relate to them, get the answers, organize everything and draw your conclusions on the material collected.

The critical thing when carrying out this kind of search is to stay focused and have the patience to dig out customers' spontaneous discussions on your research topic.

This process is also useful for answering critical questions about products that are still under development or are scheduled to be developed. Often a new product or service can be improved before its launch by carrying out online research into the key elements that led to it being designed. As they say in marketing: "First, find out whether dogs actually eat the dog food."

## SEARCH YOUR MEDIA

Searching for your media is very important so that you know which blogs, websites, and forums are relevant to your business and your customers. You will use this list as your basis for media tracking, advertising, viral campaigns, and online search.

You will use your online media search to create a media map, a classified list of the media you have identified as being worthwhile to interact with, whether for running ads, sending press releases or submitting articles about your company.

To carry out your media search, start by searching in Google, forums and social networks that are relevant to your customers. Use keywords related to your business for this purpose. For example, if you are in the business of selling sports shoes, search for words such "shoes" "walking shoes" or "Nike shoes." Think like your customer.

After an initial search, classify these media according to their relevance and focus, checking which have the best positions in Google searches.

List everything in a spreadsheet and sort the websites and blogs according to their focus and relevance to your business. Those at the top of the list will be those that appear most frequently and in the best positions in your searches.

Once your list is finalized, contact each of the sites and blogs for information about advertising options and costs and add these to your spreadsheet. This worksheet will then become your guide for planning where and when to advertise, how much to spend, and with which media you should build your relationships by sending press releases and articles about your business, products, and services.

## KEEP AN EYE ON YOUR COMPETITORS

It is crucial that your company offers to its customers excellent quality and competitive products and services. But to be a leader you need to stay one step ahead of the competition. In business, the winner is not necessarily the best, but the one who heads in the right direction before the rest of the pack.

Knowing where your competitors are, what they are doing online and how they are implementing their digital activities is essential to achieve and maintain leadership.

Moreover, the most efficient way to learn is from other people's mistakes and successes. Knowing what your competitors are doing is the best way to avoid making mistakes and discover what gets the best results.

So, watch and research your competitors continually. Visit their websites and understand what they are doing on the Internet: do they have online sales? Are they are carrying out digital marketing activities? Are they well positioned in Google search?

Use keywords such as your competitors' brand name or themes related to their businesses. Do some research and note down where you come across them and where they are positioned concerning you.

Keep these results and compare them every month, trimester or semester with the latest results from the same search. This will show you and your competitors, and you are evolving on the Internet.

Visit the competitors' sites and analyze how they are using content and layout and whether they are selling online.

If you sell online, analyze your sales process and how efficient it is. Buy products from your competitors' stores and study the entire shopping experience. Look at the advantages and problems, and learn from them.

Find your competitors in social networks and follow them. What are they posting? How are they building their networking? What promotions or campaigns are they running? What customer return rates do they have?

Remember: The most important thing is to be the best at what you do – which means doing things better than your competitors are doing them.

## MAKE CLIPPINGS

In addition to searching for information about your customer's opinion, the online media, and your competitors, you need to stay informed. Subscribe to a free or paid electronic clipping service, focusing on keywords related to your business.

Remember the importance of always keeping in touch with what is happening on the Internet about your business. This will help you identify good opportunities, anticipate your competitors' actions and recognize the arrival of new competitors or threats to your business quickly.

## NEXT STEP

You learned the sixth step, to search, to build knowledge as a competitive advantage. You learned how to do online research and how to search your customer's opinions, the best online media for your business and how to search your competitor's online actions.

Next, we will show the seventh step, to track your online actions, monitoring, analyzing and learning from them.

# STEP 7 - TRACK

## MONITOR, ANALISE AND LEARN

The final and seventh step is to track your online actions, monitoring, analyzing and learning from them.

One of the advantages of digital marketing is that its results can be tracked and measured. Tracking is the step that integrates the results of all other steps, allowing you to verify the results and act for correcting directions or improving actions. It occurs in a variety of ways, including monitoring, assignment, and conversion.

Monitoring collects information about visits to a website or downloads from an app. The online search can use monitoring to gather information to complement the research and also compare search findings with the results of marketing actions. Online media and social networks monitoring measures not only results, but also brand image, consumer opinion, product and service issues, and various other information about your company.

The assignment allows you to identify and assign each user visit, access or action to a given partner, agent or identity. This is very important when assigning the weight of results and investments in advertising, or creating an affiliate campaign where other consumers have advantages in referring friends to your business.

Finally, the conversion tracks the actual commercial result, the sale, of a product or service. It is critical in online sales actions, but also very useful for analyzing the conversation of your digital investments in leads and offline sales.

Tracking is, in fact, the combination of digital activities aimed at tracking the results of strategies and actions that have already been implemented, to improve outcomes and efficiency.

The golden rule here is "if it cannot be measured, it cannot be improved." Tracking is a core step. It involves monitoring your website, your blog and all your digital activities, understanding the results, setting targets, improving what is not working, and reinforcing what is.

So, in addition to implementing the six steps outlined so far in this practical guide, it is essential that you monitor your website and all your digital activities to measure the outcomes and learn from them.

Any business should carry out at least a minimum tracking so that they can analyze the results of their digital activities easily and quickly. In the following pages, we will look at the track you should keep for your business online.

## MONITOR YOUR SITE RIGHT NOW

Use a website-monitoring tool. If you do not already have one, start with Google Analytics, which is free. This tool will enable you to monitor all your web pages, generate reports for each individual page and for the site as a whole for particular days, weeks, months and other specific periods.

With this tool, be it Google Analytics or any other, you should be able to monitor your own site traffic with daily reports.

Pay attention to the following specific points when monitoring your site:

1. The number of visits: The total number of site visits is your website's primary indicator.

2. Number of Visitors: This indicates your site audience, i.e., how many people actually visited your site. Remember that a person may visit your website more than once; so, for instance, your number of visits in a month could be ten thousand while your number of individual visitors might be five thousand.

3. The number of pages per visit: This measures how relevant your site is to its visitors. Each time a person visits your site, they may view a single page or go on to see dozens of them. The higher the number of pages viewed per visit, the more people are actually exploring the information it contains.

4. List of most visited pages: This indicates the number of visits received by each individual page. You can then use this list to analyze which themes, products or

information grab your customers' attention the most. It also includes your campaign landing pages, providing you with final stats for each of your marketing initiatives.

5. Length of visit: This indicates how long on average your visitors stayed on your site, thus showing how well they relate to your content. The longer your visitors stay, the higher their interest.

6. Origin of visitors: This identifies which site your visitors originated from, i.e., where your customer was immediately before visiting your site. Generally these are classified according to: direct visits, in which customers enter your web address directly in their browser; site referrals, in which a visitor comes to your site after clicking on a link in another website, blog or social network; and search engines, in which a visitor finds your website by clicking on a link in Google or another search engine.

## MONITOR EACH ACTIVITY

Create a separate landing page for every digital marketing initiative. Knowing where your visitors have come from means, you can monitor specific activities

For every new digital marketing campaign or activity, create a dedicated landing page with a unique address such as www.yoursite.com/promo.php. By doing this, you will be able to analyze each action independently.

Define what information will be monitored in the campaign. This will usually be information that affects its development or is related to its objectives.

Define what conversion rate you are aiming for according to your campaign objective, and create a conversion page.

## USE ONE TRACK FOR EACH STEP

For each digital marketing step or action, there is a set of necessary information that should be monitored.

For the talk, you track your content, monitor each blog post using the same tracking information that you use for your site.

For interact, you track the origin of the visits, separating out each source, i.e., whether the visitor came via Twitter or Facebook, and where they go next, for example, whether they spend some time on your site or leave from the same page they entered. Also track the size of your contact network, its growth and the volume of comments, shares, retweets, and likes obtained for each of your social media actions.

For tell step, use a tracking mechanism to check which emails or other instant messages are opened and which resulted in visits to your site or campaign page. To do this, use an image uploaded to your site and links, detailing the information contained in the message. Many platforms provide email tracking mechanisms that can be incorporated into the email message.

For the spread, including a tracking point in the text, widget or video to measure the number of downloads, views or clicks it receives. Monitor visits, length of stay and number shares.

For push you track the number of clicks and amount of time spent on the site, using a separate landing page for each format.

For any social media or social network action, you can also use its embedded monitoring tools. Monitor the number of views, shares, likes and time spent.

## REGULAR ANALYSIS

Organize a periodic review of the information you monitor. Set up a weekly or monthly meeting and analyze all the data observed. Look at what progress has been made compared to the previous period and what was better or worse.

At the end of each review meeting, make a list of actions to be implemented to correct or improve the aspects you have analyzed. Set goals to be reached before the next meeting, usually, a percentage increase concerning the numbers analyzed.

Whenever you are implementing an online advertising or viral campaign, set a regular time, ideally on a weekly basis, for analyzing your monitoring information and making decisions about how to change course where necessary. Allow for at least four analyses during the campaign.

At the end of the campaign, make a general analysis of the results and try to learn from the mistakes, successes and customer behavior exhibited.

If you are disciplined about the implementation of your actions for tracking, monitoring and analyzing results, not only will you achieve better results from your digital marketing, you will also be more secure when investing in future activities.

## NEXT STEP

You learned the seventh step, to track your online actions, monitoring, analyzing and learning from them. And you learned that you can track for a variety of goals, including monitoring, assignment, and conversion.

Remember tracking is a core step, and the golden rule is "if it cannot be measured, it cannot be improved."

Now that you learn all the seven steps that will allow you to engage your customers, get new ones, increase your sales, and build a winning digital marketing strategy.

But we will end this practical guide giving you a bonus chapter to help you to improve your digital identity and presence. Enjoy it.

# AN EXTRA STEP

## BEFORE YOU START

So far we have discussed the seven steps that will allow you to engage your customers, get new ones, increase your sales, and build a winning digital marketing strategy. These seven steps were developed to help you make the most of your investment in the Internet and social networks.

But within the world of business, we assume that many already have established a robust digital presence. But that is not always true. And many times, a company, brand or professional considers having an excellent digital presence, but don´t.

I will, therefore, devote a bonus chapter to you check actions that your company needs to take to be sure you have a strong digital identity and presence, essential before implementing any of the steps you learned.

Consider this a checklist. If after reading you find something missing, fix it. If you don´t, that is great.

At this point, you may be wondering why we started with the seven steps, once is a must to have an established digital identity and presence beforehand. The main reason is that once you understand what you must do and what you can gain by using the seven steps, you will have the motivation to make the necessary adjustments to your digital identity and presence.

So, this part of this book will cover the basics of a company's digital identity and presence. It is essential that you read this chapter carefully to be sure that your own digital identity and presence is satisfactory.

Businesses vary enormously regarding their digital identity and presence. Some companies still have no web or email at all and therefore need to establish a digital identity before starting work on their online marketing.

Others maybe have a small website, a profile on a social network, a Blogger or WordPress blog and an email account on Gmail. This is still less than minimal at the today's market.

And finally, there are those who believe they have a good website and an adequate presence. Even so, you should read this chapter carefully as I am sure there will be some surprises.

If you have friends whose business still does not have a domain, website or email, do them a favor and give them this book as a gift.

## YOUR BUSINESS DIGITAL IDENTITY

A company's digital identity is entirely different from an individual's identity. If you as a person just use Gmail to communicate with your friends, it is fine, but this is not the case for a company.

There are millions of consumers using the Internet, and they will judge your business by your company digital identity. You may have a fantastic company, great products or services, but online customers will only discover that through your digital identity. If they do not like or feel confident with your company's online identity, they can make the wrong impression of your company and end up not doing business with you.

Think of your digital business identity as your business card or your shop showcase or storefront. Imagine for example that you own a store and rather than your customers having contact via the Internet, they only have contact via your storefront. In this case, it doesn't matter if your resources are limited, you must guarantee that your storefront has a good presence that makes your customers feel comfortable, understand what you do and build a good impression of your shop.

## YOUR DOMAIN

To begin building your digital identity, you need an Internet domain, which is basically your name on the Internet. The domain is the famous www.yourname.com that you have already heard so much about. Do not set up a Gmail address with your company name – your customers will not take you seriously if you cannot spend ten dollars on your own domain name. Not only that but it can lead them to believe that you are a scammer.

So, hire an Internet service provider and create a unique domain for your company. Most providers offer inexpensive packages for domain and hosting.

As you will probably discover, you cannot always create a domain with the exact name of your company, so be creative. For example, if you have a restaurant named Taste, you will probably have to create your domain as www.tasterestaurant.com. This is no problem, choose any name that is easy to spell and have some relation to your company but makes sure your company has a domain.

Also, usually when you create your unique domain (www.tasterestaurant.com), you will also gain access to a set of unique emails too (name@tasterestaurant.com).

## YOUR WEBSITE

There is no reason why your company should not have a website. To have a site, no matter how simple it is, is vital for any business. If you have nothing in place, contract a set of a basic webpage with four or five pages that describe your company, its products and services and contains a contact page.

If you do not have a website, millions of customers do not even know you exist. Also if you have a small business in a small town, you have to have a site. This is how thousands of customers in your city will find you.

For small businesses, in particular, you could consider substituting a site with your own Wordpress blog. Many

Internet providers already provide free with your account a version of WordPress that is quick and easy to install. A blog is basically a site that can be updated without any technical assistance, with the added benefits that it can be used for your content and tailor its layout to appeal to your target audience.

This way you create your own domain, create your company's email addresses, host your site and install WordPress, building your digital identity with one hosting company for a single monthly fee.

So, to summarize – there is no excuse for not having your own domain and website.

## DIGITAL COMMUNICATION

Contrary to popular belief, digital communication is useful for any business. From medium and large enterprises that have plenty of resources to throw after old communication methods, to small businesses that need to be competitive and keep their costs to a minimum to survive.

Yet in practice, tools such as WhatsApp, Skype, Zoom, and Messenger are rarely used by many businesses.

So, in addition to establishing your domain and site, I would recommend that you create a minimum digital communication platform for your company. This will make you more flexible and, above all, significantly reduce your communication costs.

The following tools I will mention form the basis of today's digital communication. So, let us take a look at how you should work with each.

## E-MAIL

Email represents the least Internet communication tool you should have in place. Along with your new domain, which we discussed earlier, you will be provided with one or more email accounts such as you@yourdomain.com. Use at least one of these accounts for your business activities.

It is essential that customers are able to communicate with your company via an email with your domain. Forget free alternatives such as Gmail, Hotmail or Yahoo. These could be good for your personal use, but they do not provide the minimum presence that a customer will expect from a professional organization.

If you have several employees who have contact with customers, give one email to each. It is critical that your customer feels comfortable communicating with your company and your employees directly.

## SKYPE

We are not talking here about changing your company's main telephone number. A mobile or a fixed line telephone is still the most common to use.

However, for long distance calls and speaking with people outside your city, or even within it, Skype is the best solution. Skype is available free on the Internet, which requires only a notebook or a smartphone.

The most significant advantage of Skype is that you can talk free of charge with others who have Skype. So, you can speak with partners, affiliates, distributors or even customers without spending a cent on phone calls or move yourself for a meeting.

You can also use Skype for calls to regular phones by buying credit called SkypeOut. This enables you to speak long distance for close to the cost of a local call.

Seriously consider using this alternative in your company and making it a part of your digital identity strategy.

## MESSENGER

Messenger is often associated with the younger generation. However, it is a great communication tool and, thanks to its broad reach, can be used to significant effect in business. It is very common to find companies and customers with Messenger, and you can use it to offer your customers a direct channel of communication with you.

Messenger also allows you to send and receive files and create groups, which can be used for everyday communications by businesses whose employees and businesses partners are geographically scattered.

Instead of sending a file as an email attachment and be left wondering whether it has been received, Messenger allows you to post it online and communicate directly with its recipient, leaving you in no doubt.

## WHATSAPP

WhatsApp is mostly used for personal communications, but more and more professionals and organizations are using WhatsApp groups to easy communicate for projects or specific tasks.

The great thing about WhatsApp is that you need only your smartphone and that you can create one group for each company projects or activities, involving just the people you need, and guarantee a fluid team communication.

## STORAGE

Although not strictly a communication feature, image storage services (like Flickr or Google photos), presentation services (such as Slideshare), videos (such as Vimeo) and files (such as Dropbox), are handy for communication via websites, social networks, email, Skype, WhatsApp or Messenger and are an addition that should be used in your company.

Uploading your pictures, videos, presentations to the Internet not only saves you time but also creates a more professional image of your business, enabling you to send your customers links to the stored files instead of huge files to their inbox.

Furthermore, it will centralize your files, making the latest versions readily accessible by you, your marketing and sales personnel and your customers.

A further advantage is that tools such as Flickr, Vimeo, and Slideshare are also social media platforms on their own. You can use them to post files or embed them in your site, providing features such as a business presentation or its portfolio ready for viewing by customers looking for a company such as yours.

## USING GOOGLE

We cannot talk about digital presence without discussing Google. Google has a plethora of tools, some of which are vital to guarantee your presence on the Internet.

There are many useful tools in Google, and I recommend it to you explorer for a while and find the most suitable for your business.

To give you an example, if your business depends on a physical store, restaurant or office, register the name and description of your company and its subsidiaries on Google Maps. People are increasingly using Google Maps as a means of finding restaurants, shops, and even offices. So Google Maps become a complement to define your digital identity and presence better.

## DIGITAL MARKETING ACTIVITIES

Once you have created your digital identity, your domain and website, your email, Skype, WhatsApp and Messenger communication, your files uploaded in the proper storage, you need to start planning. Think about how to implement a basic online presence, and the best way to do that is to go through each one of the seven steps and execute an action out of it. But the bottom line is the first three steps, talk, interact and tell.

Choose a particular time on a specific day of the week that suits you. You need to be disciplined, so it is better to allocate the time than to try to make time each week according to your itinerary. Allow two hours on your chosen day, at your selected time to carry out the following digital activities:

> 1. Begin with Talk step, creating a blog that will be easy to update and will position your company better in the search engines. Set aside an hour a week to use this blog to write about your company, your products and services, and your business.

> 2. Them you can go for the Tell step, and ensure the site has at least one contact page, and a newsletter signs up and makes sure you respond to any contacts you receive.

> 3. Make a point of sending a newsletter once a week or two with the latest news and information about your business. At the end of the e-mail, ask your customers to forward the message to their contacts and friends.

4. Finally, go for Interact step, creating accounts for your company on Google, Twitter, and Facebook. You can always go for other social networks.

5. Search for your customers on Google, Twitter, and Facebook. Try to find blogs on the Internet and customer communities on Facebook where you can talk about your market and your business area.

6. Use your Facebook profile to participate in communities related to your business and your target audience. Participate in forums and discussion group and invite consumers of interest to be friends. Always include the name of your company, your website and your email in your signature.

7. Use your LinkedIn profile to find and communicate with people connected to your business, such as partners, consultants, and competitors. Join groups that interest you.

8. Act now, because tomorrow will be too late.

## LOOKING AFTER YOUR SITE

One thing is to have a website, but another is to have a website that works and presents a good impression of your company to your target audience. This may seem obvious, but it is surprising how many problems I come across on companies' websites that they have not noticed.

Most entrepreneurs do not answer yes to all these questions: Have you ever browsed your company's website?

Have you looked at every page? Have you done so in the last three months?

I undertook a survey of competitor sites for a client, which showed that:

> 1. Only 5% of sites surveyed could be classified as very good.
>
> 2. About 30% of sites were considered fair or, but there were layout problems, incorrect or outdated information, broken links, and inaccessible pages.
>
> 3. Another 60% of sites were classified as weak due to essential issues with navigation, significant errors, illegible text, and other serious problems.
>
> 4. And 5% of sites surveyed were almost impossible to navigate due to anti-virus blocking, because they were so slow to load or because they were so full of errors that it was impossible to work your way around.

Your company's website is its business card, its virtual storefront. When your customers visit your site, they are looking above all for speed, clarity, and quality information. Speed because they are familiar with Google, YouTube, and Facebook, where everything is speedy. Clarity because of the lack of personal contact when accessing a site leaves little room for mistakes. Your customers will not have a salesperson or receptionist to speak to – it is just them and your site, and if they do not understand what you do, they will look for another company. And quality information because your customers are used to immediacy on the Internet, and they will not understand if your company can't manage to show up useful information and update it with the latest news.

## TEST, TEST, TEST

The first thing to do is always test. Test everything. The biggest problem with most companies' websites is that they are put together in a rush and without due care and end up with presentation errors that are really frustrating for visitors.

These errors range from non-existent pages to contact forms that generate errors. Mistakes are simple to find and fix but make for a really unpleasant navigation experience. My suggestion is that you ask someone, it could even be one of your customers, to navigate around the website and make a note of every error they find. You will be surprised by what they uncover.

Not everybody knows this, but different browsers are not always completely compatible with each other. Different versions of Internet Explorer behave differently, and Firefox and Safari behave differently again. Thus, it is essential that you test your site in all the most common browsers and versions.

Sites with more advanced functions such as complicated registration, loyalty programs or social networks need more attention still. I know of companies that have carried out significant campaigns only to discover later that the records contained errors and inconsistencies, which invalidated all the results.

Remember: Test everything. Always.

## ONLINE STORES

Online stores are another problem for testing. It is incredible how many e-commerce I come across on the Internet that just does not work correctly. In general, it is not the glaring errors that are a problem, but details that prevent purchase our do not generate sufficient confidence for the customer to close the deal.

So, the rule is either to have a complete online store that generates sufficient customer confidence, or not to have one at all. It is better to have a contact phone number or a form for requesting quotes than to create e-commerce with no payment options or which, after completing all the purchase information, displays a message saying that the company will contact you to complete the purchase.

Make sure also that the buying process is clear to the client from the beginning. Nobody wants to start a purchase without knowing where it is going. So, your online store homepage needs to be very clear.

Finally, a recommendation: never post a page on your virtual store saying "coming soon" or "under construction." If you do not have a shop, just do not present that option, but do not set customer expectations that you fail to meet.

## NAVIGABILITY

Now we look at a few more conceptual and less obvious website problems. These are the worst kind because the company believes that everything is fine and does not realize that there is a problem affecting your contact with your customers.

## UNDER CONSTRUCTION

As I said before, do not use pages with phrases such as "under construction" or "coming soon." This is no longer acceptable to remove all links leading to this type of page. They waste customers' time, and they lose trust in the site links. If a page is not ready, do not link to it.

## LET THEM FIND YOU

Remember to make sure your contact information is easy to find. Do not put your email, use a simple, quick and convenient contact form. If you have commercial premises, provide your physical address. If you have phone service, give the phone number. If neither of these is essential, for instance, you work as a consultant, just create a contact form.

## QUICK REGISTERS

If you set up a registration page on your site, either for contact or for a newsletter, keep the required information to a minimum. Creating long registration forms that ask your customers for lots of personal information will send them away. The idea is to ask for name and email and nothing more. If you need additional information, make it optional, not mandatory.

## QUICK NAVIGATION

Test your site and make sure you can get anywhere on it within just a few clicks. We are talking here about an average of two clicks and a maximum of three to access most of your site contents. If it needs more than that, rethink it entirely.

## READABLE TEXT

Be careful what fonts you are using for your text and make sure there is a proper contrast between the text and background. There are websites virtually impossible to read because the letter and background colors are similar. When building your site check that it is readable in a standard computer.

Also, take care with text formatting. Paragraphs, spaces, headings, and subheadings are essential for making reading easy.

Think about embedded text links too. They should help users access more details about the text and facilitate navigation of the site. Use text links as necessary.

Never use images instead of text, or text in a PDF or Flash file format. This makes reading difficult, slow the site down and does not allow search engines to read and index the content. All text must be actual text.

Spelling and grammar are vital. Review all your text very carefully.

### EASY MENUS

The same applies to your website menus which should clearly display their options. Another common problem with menus is over-creativity or a lack of common sense resulting in menus that are so hard to see or understand that users have no idea where to click.

I know an agency whose website has a floating menu that appears when the mouse is in certain positions on the screen. Making beautiful and creative sites does not require the making of bizarre menus. First and foremost, your website must be navigable by anyone.

Like menus, links of any kind should look like links. Complicated solutions with different shapes and colors confuse Internet users and hinder navigation.

## NO POP-UPS OR TRAPS

If there is one thing that Internet users hate, it is popups, windows that the site opens automatically. These windows hinder navigation, irritate users and do not achieve anything. There is no plausible reason to use pop-ups on your site so just do not do it.

Moreover, as technology has advanced, some developers have tried to force the inclusion of cookies, or ways to track Internet navigation. Most of these end up being blocked by antivirus software and prevent navigation of your site.

Even worse, in some cases, it can cause Google itself to list your website as untrusted and what seemed like a great idea can turn into a nightmare. So, beware of promises to deliver detailed information about users as these can jeopardize access to your site.

## ATTRACTIVE DESIGN

You may not be good at design or have hired a professional to make your site, but you probably have good instincts and know someone with good taste.

The graphic design of a site makes a big difference to how customers see your business. Sites with old, unpleasant or confusing design will give customers the impression that your company is outdated, uncomfortable and confusing.

Make sure the design of your site is at least pleasant. If you do not know how to do this yourself and do not have the money to hire a designer, take my advice: make a straightforward site based on WordPress and choose a nice attractive template style. There are hundreds to choose from at Wordpress.org.

If on the other hand, you already have a website, here is some advice for avoiding common design errors that can cost your business and undermine your company's image.

## WELL-DISTRIBUTED DESIGN

A website's design should be well organized. Being overly inventive can be a problem. The gold area of a site is the top left corner and top center, and this is where you should focus the initial messages that you want to convey to customers.

Do not let the site's image header take up too much space. On some websites this image occupies more than 70% of the screen, requiring customers to scroll down to see the content.

Browse other sites and find a balance that suits you, then use this as a reference for building your own your site

## CALM DESIGN

Beware of objects moving on the screen, flashing images and other features that look creative but give your customers eyestrain. The site's purpose is not to prove that you can do amazing things with programming, but to create a calm environment that makes it pleasant for clients to navigate your site. So movement, animation, and visual effects are beautiful to use on banners but do not use them on the entire site.

## USE COLORS IN THE RIGHT PLACES

The colors used on a site should be well considered. Each color helps to create a different feeling in people so carefully think when you are deciding which to use.

The text should be easy to read, and the colors should be harmonious. Do not use too many colors or contrasting colors unless you know what you are doing and have a clear intention of stirring a different emotion in your customers.

## IMAGE QUALITY

Any image used must be of suitable quality for the Internet. Images with little resolution are not aesthetically pleasing and prejudice your site's quality, while very high-resolution images will make your site slow. Use images that are small enough to provide good resolution on a computer screen.

The majority of your images must be of sufficient quality to display well on a screen with a good resolution. Do some tests by accessing your own site to see if the images appear clearly and do not take too long to load.

## CONTENT IS KING

Remember what we said about content and look after your content and keep it up to date.

# A PRACTICAL PLAN

In this book, I have presented the seven steps that allow you to engage your customers, get new ones, increase your sales, and build a winning digital marketing strategy.

Now I will present first some tips to keep you connected and posted about the future of digital ground, and at the end of this chapter, to facilitate the implementation of these steps, I have created this easy to use plan in a checklist format for your day-to-day use.

## KEEP CONNECTED

It is impossible to know what will happen tomorrow. One cannot make firm predictions about the near future, especially concerning the Internet and digital marketing.

There is always something new and something more to learn. As I write this, Foursquare, a social network aimed at owners of restaurants and other businesses, is becoming popular and Pinterest, a social network for tagging and sharing is becoming the new star of Internet startups.

However, anticipating the next developments on the Internet, in social networks, and in digital marketing can provide businesses with enormous competitive advantage, particularly small businesses that can leverage a new service to drive and grow their business.

If, for example, you have a small business in the fashion industry and you know that Pinterest is growing fast, you can give your business a quick boost by using this new product.

The good news is that you do not need to predict the future, you just need to understand what is happening before your competitor. Keep up to date with what is going on, and you will spot consolidated trends before your competitors. That alone will keep you ahead of the market.

Follow these tips to keep up to date about the future and trends on the Internet, in digital marketing and in social media.

## KEEPING UP TO DATE WITH THE FUTURE

Create and implement the seven steps you learn in this book for keeping in constant contact with your online customers. Digital marketing activities provide a lot of information about new developments.

Create a bookmark list in your preferred browser for updates on technological innovations from social media, blogs, influencers, and other information sources. Do not use mainstream media for this. Read blogs and other online media that are actually talking about cutting-edge subjects. Check this list once a week and read the articles that most grab your attention.

Understand how customers will be able to use their phones and gadgets in the future and start thinking about how they can become an ally in your digital presence.

Watch out for Internet startups, which can appear and grow very fast, as happened with Twitter, Groupon, Dropbox, and Pinterest. If you catch one of these waves early, you can collect big rewards.

The most important thing here is to embrace Internet-related technologies and use them. This way you will better understand what lies ahead and will be well placed to come up with great ideas for your business.

## FINAL RECOMMENDATIONS

To close this book, I will give you some final recommendations:

1. Research, research, research. Carry out online research. There is information out there, so use it.

2. Plan your digital marketing activities in an integrated fashion. Think of the whole picture. We talk about seven steps so consider them all when you do your planning.

3. Participate in everything, even if only a little. It is better to run small actions in every one of the steps you learn than one significant isolated activity.

4. Listen and interact. Read blogs and participate in communities and forums. Listen to your customers and

what they are saying on the Internet. Interact with them when you feel comfortable.

5. Be sociable. Expand your network. Put yourself out there. Participate. Use the Internet to be friendly and do not hide behind your desk.

6. Always think about people. Do not be fooled. Plan your actions and carry them out with people in mind.

7. Act now, because tomorrow is too late.

# STEP 1 - TALK

[ ] Define your target audience clearly and accurately.

[ ] Plan your content according to the steps provided in this book.

[ ] Allocate the necessary resources for the planning and continuous production of your content.

[ ] Set up your blog using a tool such as WordPress.

[ ] Promote your blog regularly, helping your content to raise its profile on social networks and other blogs.

[ ] Make sure your content is relevant to your customer community, making sure you keep it regularly updated and useful for your audience.

[ ] Keep your focus and resist the temptation to mix content with advertising, thereby creating text of no interest.

[ ] Track, monitor, analyze and learn – and never forget to do this.

## STEP 2 - INTERACT

[ ] Create a blog to facilitate communication.

[ ] Create a Twitter profile. Find people who are essential to your business and follow them.

[ ] Install an application on your blog that tweets your posts, and writes about exciting things that happen to your business once a day.

[ ] Make a map of the influencers with at least fifteen blogs and influencers related to the business you are in. Subscribe and follow them once a week.

[ ] Leave comments whenever you read an interesting post. Include your email and website address in your signature.

[ ] Create a Facebook profile. Find communities that interest you and join them. Keep track of your contacts and messages once a week.

[ ] Create a professional profile on LinkedIn. Join groups that interest you and keep track of your contacts and messages once a week.

[ ] Never use a bulk-mailing tool.

[ ] Set aside a specific time, once a week to work on your relationships with the public and on social networks.

## STEP 3 - TELL

[ ] Create and maintain your own email database.

[ ] Only purchase company email lists that clearly indicate how the emails were obtained.

[ ] Establish the best days and times to send messages.

[ ] Create a registration page on your site.

[ ] Set up a standard template that is easy to read and use it with all your emails.

[ ] Create a weekly or bi-weekly newsletter with news about your business. If your company does not generate much news, includes information about your business sector.

[ ] Create "Refer a Friend" and new registration campaigns from time to time.

[ ] Only send messages that are interesting, and offers that are genuine and exclusive. Make an impact.

## STEP 4 - PUSH

[ ] Research online media to build and maintain a list of preferred advertising media for your company.

[ ] Create an interactive banner for your business. Make it something different that really calls attention. Rather than just a banner, it should be a piece that attracts customers and makes them interact with it.

[ ] Set aside a part of your advertising budget that is acceptable for your company, and use it for placing banners.

[ ] Make videos about your business. They should not advertise your company, they should reflect your customers' interests regarding your business. Aim to educate, entertain or amuse.

[ ] Create a YouTube channel with these videos and track the results. Play videos on your site or blog using YouTube tools.

[ ] If the younger generation forms part of your target market, invest in the creation of a good online game and promote it via social networks.

## STEP 5 - SPREAD

[ ] Think about a market niche that you want to target that is difficult to break into.

[ ] Research that niche and find out on which social networks it has a presence.

[ ] Search Google for three viral campaigns set up for similar niches

[ ] With your research material, brainstorm with at least five people to create ideas for viral campaigns.

[ ] Leave the brainstorm with at least one viral campaign that you think will surprise and having defined your social network, a method of seeding and profile of your alpha users.

[ ] Keep an eye out for detail with everything you produce. Be creative and make something you are proud of.

[ ] Seed your viral campaign, work your alpha users to follow the activity.

[ ] Learn from the experience. If the campaign does not generate great results, try to analyze why so that you can get the next one right. If the results are satisfactory, well done, keep going. If it is a great success, produce a case study and publish it to inspire others.

## STEP 6 - SEARCH

[ ] Define a set of at least three key questions that when answered can create a competitive advantage for your business.

[ ] Carry out an online survey to answer these questions, remembering these five steps: formulate questions, define your sources, define your media, define your keywords and implement your search.

[ ] Carry out Internet research as de

scribed in this book. Interact with your list of classified media, run ads and send them press releases about your company to be written up in these media.

[ ] Research your competitors, including their website, online store, search engine results position and digital marketing activities.

[ ] Repeat your competitor research every quarter or at least every six months.

[ ] Subscribe to a free or paid electronic clipping service, for keywords related to your business.

## STEP 7 - TRACK

[ ] Use a site-monitoring tool such as Google or Facebook Analytics.

[ ] Maintain general site monitoring with reports and a monthly review meeting.

[ ] Create a new landing page for every campaign.

[ ] Define what information will be monitored in the campaign.

[ ] Define what conversion you are aiming for based on your campaign objective and create a conversion page.

[ ] For email marketing campaigns, put a tracking point in place, so you know which emails have been opened.

[ ] For viral marketing campaigns, establish a tracking point for downloads, views or clicks.

[ ] Define how regularly you will analyze the tracking information and make decisions about course correction during the campaign.

[ ] At the end of the campaign, produce a general analysis of the results so that you can learn from your mistakes, successes and customer behavior during the campaign.

# WHERE NEXT?

During my work I spend hours surfing the Internet and looking for information to enrich the content of my books. Books usually include a bibliography of the written works that served as references for their author. However, as this book is about digital marketing, I must create a bibliography dedicated to the many texts, sites and information sources that I used to produce it.

So, I have created a digital bibliography of the references I used, online rather than printed so that it is of more use to you for your own research.

As the Internet changes all the time, I will also publish updated versions of the digital bibliography on my website

WWW.THEDIGITALENABLERS.COM

You can also subscribe for free to The Digital Enablers Club and receive updated information and additional materials about digital marketing and the seven steps to enable your business to engage your customers, get new ones, increase your sales, and build a winning digital marketing strategy.

WWW.THEDIGITALENABLERS.COM/CLUB

# SOCIAL MEDIA NETWORKS

Social media networks are in a constant state of evolution. Internet users maintain profiles and participate in one or more networks, as well as reading or being members of other social media.

- LinkedIn (www.linkedin.com)
- Twitter (www.twitter.com)
- Facebook (www.facebook.com)
- MySpace (www.myspace.com)
- YouTube (www.youtube.com)
- Slideshare (www.slideshare.net)
- Flickr (www.flickr.com)

## COLLABORATIVE WEBSITES

On collaborative sites, the users themselves create the content. This model has grown tremendously, especially in areas related to innovation, science, and technology.

- Innocentive (www.innocentive.com)
- IstockPhoto (www.istockphoto.com).
- Yahoo Respuestas (br.answers.yahoo.com).
- LEGO Factory (factory.lego.com)
- CrowdSpirit (www.crowdspirit.com)

# LINK AGGREGATORS

Link aggregators, also called social bookmarks, service through which Internet users save their sites. These are similar to your browser favorites, but other Internet users can read them and vote.

- Delicious (www.delicious.com)
- Dihitt (www.dihitt.com)
- StumbleUpon (www.stumbleupon.com)
- Favoritus (www.favoritus.com)
- Digg (www.digg.com)
- Linkto (www.linkto.com)
- Reddit (www.reddit.com)
- Linkk (www.linkk.com)

# OPEN SOURCE

Open source software is highly useful for building sites, blogs and portals. They should be your first port of call for a solution for your site.

- WordPress (www.wordpress.org)
- Magento (www.magentocommerce.org)
- Wiki (www.wiki.org)
- V-Tiger (www.vtiger.com)
- PHPBB (www.phpbb.com)
- PHPlist (www.phplist.com)
- OpenX (www.openx.org)
- PhpIzabi (www.phpizabi.net)

# OTHER REFERENCE SOURCES

Specific sites are excellent references for any work on the Internet. These include the leading search engines and any specific portals that are of significant reference in your sector.

- Google (www.google.com)
- Yahoo (www.yahoo.com)
- Wikipedia (www.wikipedia.com)
- Technorati (www.technorati.com)
- Creatives Commons (www.creativecommons.org).

# ADDITIONAL MATERIAL

You can get additional digital marketing materials and articles, as well new books on our my website

WWW.THEDIGITALENABLERS.COM

You can also subscribe for free to The Digital Enablers Club and receive updated information and additional materials about digital marketing and the seven steps to enable your business to engage your customers, get new ones, increase your sales, and build a winning digital marketing strategy.

WWW.THEDIGITALENABLERS.COM/CLUB

# ABOUT THE AUTHOR

Claudio Torres is a senior software engineer, with a BA in Electronic Engineering, an MSc in Software Systems. His career spans more than 30 years in the software development industry, working on projects for high-profile companies like ABB, Siemens, Volvo, and Renault.

He is the author of the bestseller "Digital Marketing Bible," the book he presents a comprehensive theory and a strategic model for the use of the Internet and digital technologies in business.

He is the founder of Torres Labs, a game development studio, where he works as the lead programmer and games developer. Claudio has been part of the Unity engine game development community for 6 years and counting.

As CTO of WorldBit, he manages a global team of developers, both frontend and backend, to produce and launch WorldBit technology, based on an Ethereum token (WorldBit or WBT). WorldBit Explorer is one of his key accomplishments – an augmented-reality and geo-localization mobile game-like application, that's focused on creating a worldwide marketplace using Ethereum and cryptocurrency technology.